Easy
INDIAN
cooking

Suneeta Vaswani

Robert
ROSE

For complete cataloguing information, see page 185.

Disclaimer
The recipes in this book have been carefully tested by our kitchen and our tasters. To the best of our knowledge, they are safe and nutritious for ordinary use and users. For those people with food or other allergies, or who have special food requirements or health issues, please read the suggested contents of each recipe carefully and determine whether or not they may create a problem for you. All recipes are used at the risk of the consumer.

We cannot be responsible for any hazards, loss or damage that may occur as a result of any recipe use.

For those with special needs, allergies, requirements or health problems, in the event of any doubt, please contact your medical adviser prior to the use of any recipe.

Design & Production: PageWave Graphics Inc.
Editor: Carol Sherman
Copy Editor: Julia Armstrong
Recipe Testing: Jennifer MacKenzie
Photography: Mark T. Shapiro
Food Styling: Kate Bush
Prop Styling: Charlene Erricson
Color Scans: Colour Technologies

Cover image: Fragrant Rice Layered with Curried Chicken
            (Hyderabadi Chicken Biriyani) (page 42)

We acknowledge the financial support of the Government of Canada through the Book Publishing Industry Development Program (BPIDP) for our publishing activities.

Published by Robert Rose Inc.
120 Eglinton Avenue East, Suite 800, Toronto, Ontario, Canada M4P 1E2
Tel: (416) 322-6552 Fax: (416) 322-6936

Printed in Canada
2 3 4 5 6 7 8 9 10 FP 11 10 09 08 07 06

Easy
INDIAN
cooking

Contents

✽ ✽ ✽

Acknowledgments

This book is the result of 25 years of teaching Indian cooking and is due in great part to the enthusiasm and support of my hundreds of students. What started as a hobby in 1977 quickly grew into a fulfilling career, and along the way not only enabled me to proudly explain and demonstrate the foods of India, but also led to another exciting occupation, that of tour guide to the land of my birth.

Although the list of people who have supported me in this endeavor would fill several pages, I am particularly grateful to the small band of devoted students in Houston who have been with me for the past 14 years and are now more my muses. They have come to every class I have taught in my own cooking school and presented me with the challenge of coming up with 60 to 70 new dishes each year. I am referring to Margaret Hutchings, Julia Edwards, Bettie Long, Virginia Gray, Renate Wolter and Michelle Zaniewski-Singh, among others. To Toni Allegra, I owe a huge debt. Her unwavering faith and constant inspiration kept me going and made me believe that this book would be a reality. Her gentle spirit and her faith in my abilities inspired me to keep writing, even when I felt inadequate. I am also greatly indebted to Bill Wallace, who gave me an entrée into the world of elite cooking schools, to Bob Nemerovski, whose invaluable insight has helped me to fine-tune menus to suit the diverse cooking schools, and to Cathy Cochran Lewis, who gave me the opportunity to spread my wings in Texas.

Lisa Ekus, my tenacious agent, believed in me and worked hard to sell the book, and Carol Sherman, my wonderful editor, taught me so much and has been a delight to work with. Her cool, calm attitude helped tremendously during a crisis at the very end of the project. Bob Dees, who took a chance on an unknown author, Jennifer MacKenzie, for patiently testing recipes, Mark Shapiro and his group for the photography, and the entire gang at PageWave Graphics for creating such a beautiful book.

And then there is my family, who have encouraged and supported me in this endeavor: my grandchildren — Jai, Nina, Ashwin, Nandita, ages 5 to 10 — who were adamant their names appear in my book though some of them prefer hamburgers and chicken nuggets to my cooking; and my sons, Sanjay and Dinesh, who do prefer my cooking. I am also grateful to my sister-in-law, Suzie, and our dear friends Richard and Mercedes Dewey, who have patiently tasted and critiqued many of my offerings. I also thank my daughters-in-law: Preeti, who is arguably one of the most creative and gifted cooks I have known, and who has shared many a mouth-watering recipe with me; and Susan, whose encouragement over the years has meant so much. And last but certainly not the least, my husband, Nanik, whose editorial skills were called upon frequently, and whose incredible patience, support and encouragement helped in no small measure to make this book possible.

Introduction

India, the land of my birth, from which I am unable to cut the umbilical cord, is an enigma. Try as I might, I cannot describe it in a sentence, a paragraph or even a page.

I have spent approximately half my life in India and am still continually learning about my people, the traditions and the food. The last, I'm convinced, is more than one lifetime's project — it is so vast and so diverse. Within each state, there are several different communities, each with its own cuisine. Until television became mainstream, communities lived in relative isolation, unaware for the most part of the food traditions of their neighbors. Today, television has changed the lives of Indians. Food shows on TV have raised awareness of the diversity of our cuisine in every village, where even illiterate grandmothers watch mesmerized as celebrity chefs prepare dishes from different regions.

Indian food has evolved over centuries, influenced by history, geography and religious beliefs. The greatest impact on the food of north India undoubtedly came from the Moguls, who ruled from the 16th century until the middle of the 18th century. Theirs was a sophisticated and refined cuisine, and they introduced ingredients such as saffron, nuts and cream.

The Europeans, beginning with the Portuguese — who arrived in 1498 on the southwest coast of Kerala in search of pepper, the black gold — also left their mark on the food of India. They brought with them foods from the New World — ingredients such as tomatoes, potatoes and peppers, which are synonymous with Indian food today. The British, who were the most dominant of the western powers, ruled the country for nearly three centuries and left their mark on its food. Indian spices changed British taste buds forever, and the British, in return, introduced Indians to processed cheese, breaded fried foods and the ubiquitous "baked dish," usually a medley of vegetables in a "white sauce," which still appears on party tables today. Sandwiches and white bread are also a legacy of the British, and Indians have taken both to new heights, making white bread a staple in the Indian diet.

The food of the north is completely different from that of the south. In the north, wheat is the main staple, as are other grains, such as millet and sorghum; flatbreads made from these are relished with gusto. Of course, rice is also very much a part of the diet, and the famous basmati rice is grown in the north. In the south, rice rules: more than 20 varieties are grown in the area. It is served in multiple courses at each meal, including breakfast, while wheat plays a very small role. Spices are used in all Indian food but are treated differently. In most cases, people in north India toast certain spices and grind them into a powder. These are then added individually to dishes in varying quantities during cooking. In southern cooking, spices are often combined and fried in a teaspoon of oil, then powdered and added to a dish almost at the end of the cooking process.

In *Easy Indian Cooking*, I have included recipes from northern and southern cuisines as well as those from some of the other regions of India. In this way, I hope to give you some idea of the vast diversity of the food of India.

— Suneeta Vaswani

GENERAL GUIDELINES

Cookware and Tools

Indian cooking does not require a lot of special equipment, but a few essentials make it easier. Wide-bottomed pans with tight-fitting lids are a must so that foods brown evenly from contact with the pan and the moisture in the foods will condense inside the lid and drip back into the pan to cook the food without adding more liquid. This intensifies the flavors. Stockpots do not work very well for Indian cooking.

I prefer good-quality nonstick cookware, which necessitates minimal fat, usually about a quarter of what's called for in a traditional recipe. Even though this small amount is not always adequate to "fry" foods like onions, it is acceptable to augment the oil with spoonfuls of water or stock to help the onions brown to the desired degree. This process requires a little more "pot watching," but the end results are worth the extra effort to retain the authenticity of the flavors with considerably less fat.

In recent years, several good brands of heatproof silicone spatulas have appeared on the market. I find these invaluable as they allow you to stir into the curve of the pot.

COMMON INGREDIENTS

An organized kitchen is the key to a positive kitchen experience. Stock it with basic ingredients to make your cooking adventures hassle-free.

Beans and Legumes

Kidney beans, chickpeas (canned or dried), lentils (whole masoor), Indian black beans (sabat urad), green mung beans (sabat mung), red lentils (masoor dal), split yellow peas (channa dal), yellow lentils (toor dal), yellow mung beans (mung dal) and split white beans (urad dal). Beans and dals should be stored in airtight containers.

Breads

Chapati and puri are the daily bread of Indians. Both are made of the same whole wheat dough and are used to scoop up morsels of food. Chapati is a flatbread; puri is a light, puffy deep-fried bread.

Tandoori breads and naan are made by patting the dough between the palms and expertly slapping each piece into the neck of the tandoor, a large clay-shaped vessel that is buried in the ground (see Meats, page 11, for more information). Instantly, gravity pulls the lower half of the bread, resulting in the teardrop shape that is characteristic of naan. These cook very quickly and are best eaten fresh and hot. Unfortunately, the tandoor is not common in most households, and the best one can do is to use a charcoal grill for tandoori recipes. You can also purchase ready-made breads in Indian stores or some large supermarkets.

Cilantro (see Herbs, page 18)

Clarified butter (see Oil and Ghee)

Extracts

A commonly used ingredient in special rice dishes and in sweets is rose essence (extract). It is concentrated and has an indefinite shelf life. It is not to be confused with rose water, which, being water based, loses potency over time.

Fish and Seafood

The long coast of India yields an astonishing variety of fish and seafood. Around Mumbai (formerly known as Bombay), the silvery, flounder-like fish known as pomfret, is king. Along the west coast, such local fish as salmon, mackerel and sardines are eaten with gusto. There is also a large variety of shellfish, including shrimp of all types (known as prawns in India), mussels, clams and the much prized rock lobster. In the east, near Calcutta, where the mighty Ganges River meets the Bay of Bengal, river fish are cherished, in addition to the many varieties from the bay; hilsa is the most appreciated. Bengalis, who eat fish every day, attribute their intellect and good health to their diet.

Flours

Chapati flour, which should be refrigerated if you use it only occasionally, chickpea flour (besan), all-purpose flour and cream of wheat (sooji). Cream of wheat cereal works well in most recipes.

Ghee

(see Oil and Ghee)

Ginger and Garlic

Ginger and garlic are staples in Indian cuisine. A shiny, smooth, thin-skinned "hand" of ginger indicates freshness. Fresh ginger is juicy, and as it ages, the skin becomes wrinkled and the flesh fibrous. When I find really fresh ginger and particularly fresh garlic, I process large amounts of each and store them in an airtight container in the refrigerator for up to four weeks. I do not add any oil or salt. Or you can spread the finely chopped ginger or garlic on a dish, form a ½-inch (1 cm) thick brick and score into four pieces. Freeze and transfer the frozen pieces to a resealable freezer bag to freeze for up to 12 months. As needed, scrape off the necessary amount with a sharp knife.

Alternately, keep a prepared mixture. In a food processor, combine cloves of four large heads of garlic (about 6 oz/175 g) and 2 oz (30 g) peeled gingerroot. Pulse until finely chopped but not puréed. Refrigerate, tightly closed, in a glass jar, for up to one month.

Jaggery (gur)

This is unrefined cane sugar, which is used in some lentil dishes, breads and, of course, sweets. It is rich in minerals, with a molasses-like flavor. You can substitute dark brown sugar in recipes where jaggery is called for in small quantities.

Nuts

Nuts are used in curries, rice dishes and, of course, desserts. Unprocessed nuts are available in Indian stores. Having a selection of cashews, skinned pistachios, blanched almonds and raw skinned peanuts is useful.

Oil and Ghee

Any vegetable oil is fine. I prefer canola oil, because it has a nutritional profile similar to olive oil, but any vegetable oil is suitable. Ghee is clarified butter, and several good brands are available. A teaspoon of melted ghee drizzled on steamed rice is delicious, but optional.

Papadum (Papad)

A papadum is a lentil-based cracker-like accompaniment. Papadums are made from different lentils and come in many flavors, from plain to highly spiced. While papadum is often mistaken for a bread, its role in the Indian meal is purely as a crunchy accompaniment. In North America, papadums are served in Indian restaurants accompanied by two dipping sauces: a green cilantro-based savory one, the other a sweetish brown one with a tamarind and jaggery base. This new role is a result of the ubiquitous chip and dip culture we have come to expect. Papadums can be deep-fried in very hot oil for less than 10 seconds and drained on paper towels before serving. Or toast them on an open flame by holding them with tongs and rapidly flipping back and forth until cooked, about one minute. They can also be cooked in the microwave: place two papadums between paper towels and cook on High power for 35 to 40 seconds. Once cooked, they will remain fresh for 24 hours if stored in an airtight container.

Rice

Basmati rice is a must, but all basmati rice is not created equal. Even though "basmati" is often used in a generic manner to denote extra-long-grain white rice, true basmati rice can only be cultivated in the foothills of the Himalayas, where the growing conditions and the type of soil contribute to its unique nutty flavor and unmistakable aroma. And there is certainly nothing that remotely resembles "brown basmati" rice, which is a creation of rice farmers in California and is quite unsuitable for use in Indian cooking.

It is more economical to buy large bags of basmati rice at the Indian store as you will pay the same for an 11-lb (5 kg) bag as you would for 3 lbs (1.5 kg) in a supermarket, where basmati rice is sold in a 12-oz (340 g) box. It does not spoil; in fact, aged basmati is more desirable and prized for its superior flavor. In India, basmati aged two to three years is more expensive than newly harvested rice. Look for bags or boxes that state it is a product of India or Pakistan; the growing conditions are similar.

Spices (see also page 12)

Stock the basic spices. As a rule, spices in their seed form have an almost indefinite shelf life if correctly stored. Powdered spices, on the other hand, are fragile and deteriorate with exposure to air, much like coffee and pepper. We know now that when we grind small quantities of these just before using, they are far more fragrant and flavorful. I realize that grinding spices for each dish is not practical, but I suggest a compromise. Buy only small quantities of ground aromatic spices, such as coriander, cumin and garam masala, from a reliable source where they are stored in airtight jars. Avoid buying them from bulk containers, which are exposed to air. On the other hand, coriander seeds, cumin seeds, mustard seeds, fenugreek seeds, sesame seeds and poppy seeds can be stored for a year or two. Delicate spices, such as saffron, cardamom, cloves and bay leaves, which are used primarily for their fragrance, should also be bought in small quantities. Turmeric and cayenne do not deteriorate.

Yogurt

Plain yogurt is a must. It is used extensively in marinades and for flavor and consistency. I find nonfat, low-fat and full-fat yogurt all suitable for cooking purposes, with no difference in the end result. It is necessary to stabilize yogurt with 1 tsp (5 mL) cornstarch per 1 cup (250 mL) yogurt to prevent it from curdling when heated. To prevent total separation, it is important that the yogurt be at room temperature before adding it to a dish while cooking. In most cases, if there is partial curdling in the beginning, by the time the dish is ready, the appearance is remedied.

Meats

Ovens, per se, were non-existent in India, except for the clay tandoor, a large urn-shaped clay vessel about three feet tall that is buried neck deep in the ground. Live coals are placed in the bottom, and marinated meats and poultry are skewered and placed strategically at different heights to cook. You can call this broiling, roasting or grilling, but essentially you control the cooking time and, hence the desired heat, by placing the skewers at the correct distance from the coals. The meats cooked in a tandoor are not only moist and tender, they have a flavor that cannot be duplicated.

Tandoori chicken and kababs are the signature dishes of north Indian cuisine and outstanding tandoori breads like naan, are equally prized and loved by all (see Breads, page 8).

In the Indian vocabulary, kabab is a generic word describing bite-sized foods. These can be made of meat, poultry or fish or can be vegetables. The shish kabob familiar to North Americans is just one type of kabab. "Shish" is a corruption of "sheekh," which means skewer. Other kababs can be deep-fried, grilled or baked in the traditional tandoor or oven.

Lamb

Since the most common method of cooking a meat or chicken curry is braising, it is important to use the right cut of meat. The meat of choice in most instances is young goat or mutton. This word conjures up a tough old goat in the Western mind, but nothing could be further from the truth. Lamb is a good substitute for goat meat but must be trimmed of all fat as the aroma of lamb fat is too strong. Indian people are used to meat on the bone in their dishes; the bone adds flavor and keeps the meat moist. However, since most North Americans find this awkward, it is best to use boneless pieces. Leg of lamb is the best, boned and cut into chunks. I would recommend, though, that you have the butcher cut the bone into large pieces to add to the dish as it cooks. Remove the bones before serving.

Chicken

For chicken dishes that require prolonged cooking, I like to use thighs and drumsticks. Chicken breasts are the least suitable as they get stringy and dry when braised. The beauty of braising is that the gravy has to cook and thicken slowly, so the spices and seasonings mellow and infuse the chicken with the flavors. Chicken breasts are best reserved for stir-fry dishes that are quick to prepare. One important point to remember is that Indian dishes always call for skinless chicken.

Pork

Pork is not used much in Indian food and is eaten in very small pockets of the country. I have developed some recipes because I find it marries well with Indian flavors.

SPICES, SPICE BLENDS AND HERBS

Understanding spices and herbs and their correct use is the essence of understanding Indian cuisine. Spices are derived from roots, bark, leaves, buds and seeds of plants. Most are aromatic. Some need to be roasted to release the essential oils that impart their aroma and flavor, while others need to be flash-fried in hot oil to achieve the same result. Spices play a dual role in Indian food. They not only add flavor and impart aroma and color to the dishes, but most have additional attributes as well, namely, their effect on the body. Some have a cooling effect, while others are heat producing. Understandably, appropriate ones are used during particular seasons. Some act as blood purifiers, some as digestives, and still others as antiseptics. That spices make Indian food hot is not necessarily true. Only the peppers — both black peppercorns and the various dried red peppers such as cayenne — add fire, but most spices will cause the body to perspire and thereby lower body temperature. This explains why the farther south one travels in India, the hotter the food.

Indian cuisine allows the cook to be creative, and seldom is a recipe written down with precise measurements. One of the tasks I had in my self-appointed role of translating traditional recipes into acceptable North American format was to gather recipes on my frequent trips to India from older relatives and family friends who would name ingredients and provide a concise method of preparation. There was no mention of quantities, much less precise measurements! The most I could get would be a "guestimate" or, as we say in India, "andaz." When I was fortunate enough to get a hands-on lesson, I would watch carefully to see how big a pinch and how large a fistful. Over time, I became a seasoned "eyeballer"; on returning to my kitchen in Houston, I would be able to duplicate fairly accurately the dishes I had eaten. I would then write them up with precise measurements and instructions.

Using spices and herbs correctly is essential to the success of a dish. However, there is a rationale, which, once understood, will make Indian cuisine less mysterious and daunting to the novice Indian cook. In the list that follows, I have mentioned the attributes of each spice, the most frequently used combinations, the regions each is used in, and everything else you need to know.

Spices

Asafetida (Hing)

This is the gum resin of a plant, and its use dates back to the days of the Greeks and Romans. It comes in lump form, dark brown and rocklike; in this form, it has no particular aroma. Lumps are used as a preservative, to keep weevils and bugs out of dry foods and spices that are stored for a long period. To use in a recipe, break off a pea-sized piece and crush to a powder. The powder form, pale yellow in color and packaged in small plastic containers, is more common. In this form, it is mixed with rice flour to keep it free-flowing. The powdered form has a strong, distinctive aroma, a cross between onion and garlic, which lingers and can become pervasive. However, once it is used in a dish, it blends with the other flavorings and is not offensive. The most important attribute of this spice, apart from its being used by people who eschew onions and garlic for religious reasons, is that it breaks down the indigestible entity in beans, lentils and vegetables of the cruciferous family that cause flatulence, thereby making them easy to digest.

Asafetida has an indefinite shelf life if stored tightly closed in an airtight container. If using asafetida powder, be sure to seal it well and store the container in a resealable plastic bag.

Bay Leaf (Tej Patta)

Bay leaves are usually used in rice dishes as an aromatic, most often in a combination that includes cinnamon, cloves and cardamom. The Indian bay leaf is derived from the cassia tree and is a little softer. However, I prefer to use the more readily available bay laurel leaves that are grown in California, as I find them more aromatic than the dried leaves imported from India. Store in an airtight container away from heat and replace when the aroma has dissipated.

Cardamom (Elaichi)

After saffron, green cardamom pods are the most expensive spice and one of the most important in the Indian kitchen. This three-sided pod enclosing fragrant black seeds is grown in south India. It was introduced to Saudi Arabia by Arab traders, where it is widely used as an addition to coffee. In the Indian context, cardamom is used in rice pilaf, or pulao, as it is called in India, in meat and chicken dishes, and very often in desserts and sweets. Often cardamom pods are chewed after a meal, usually with cloves, as a mouth freshener.

There are two varieties of cardamom: green, which are small, about $\frac{1}{4}$ inch (0.5 cm) long; and the large thick-skinned black variety, which is about $\frac{1}{2}$ inch (1 cm) in diameter and $\frac{3}{4}$ inch (2 cm) long. The green ones are called for in most recipes and are readily available, both as whole pods and powdered. Some Indian stores now carry cardamom seeds, and that saves time and labor when a larger quantity of seeds alone is called for. Be wary of the beautiful white puffed cardamom pods. Though they are esthetically appealing, they lack flavor because they have been bleached, a process that destroys the essential oils.

The large black cardamom pods, woody and with an earthy aroma, are only available in Indian stores and have limited use. They are usually used in certain rice and meat dishes, never in desserts. In most recipes, green pods are an acceptable substitute.

Cardamom is an essential ingredient in the famous north Indian spice blend garam masala. Look for the largest and brightest green pods available, and store in an airtight container away from light and heat. If stored properly, they will last about two years.

Carom (Ajwain, Ajowan)

Carom seeds, also referred to as lovage, resemble celery seeds in appearance but have a sharper, more pronounced bite. Their flavor is somewhat like thyme. They are used in north Indian breads and savories and in some vegetable dishes. Carom seeds are used in small quantities for flavor and as a digestive aid. Refrigerate, in a resealable freezer bag, for up to three years.

Cinnamon (Dalchini)

North Americans are familiar with the beautiful, reddish brown rolled cinnamon quills that often come neatly tied in little bundles. Used extensively in baking and as an aromatic during the holidays, cinnamon is a familiar and popular spice. It is a member of the laurel family. The cinnamon used in Indian cooking comes from the cassia tree, also a member of the laurel family. It is a dull grayish color and comes in rough, uneven pieces, some as long as 6 or 7 inches (15 to 17.5 cm). It is sweeter and softer, and easier to grind into a powder. It is an essential ingredient of garam masala (see page 18). The sticks are used in rice and meat curries, often in combination with the other aromatics, cloves and cardamom. Interestingly, Indians do not use cinnamon in desserts and sweets. That role belongs to cardamom and, occasionally, nutmeg. Store cinnamon in an airtight container away from heat and light and, if possible, grind to a powder in a spice grinder just before using to achieve maximum flavor and aroma.

Clove (Lavang or Laung)

Cloves are used whole to flavor rice and meat dishes. The powdered or ground variety is mixed with other spices in elaborate blends created for specific recipes. It, too, is an important ingredient in garam masala, and is used as an ingredient in spiced tea (masala chai) and chewed as a mouth freshener. Freshly harvested cloves are plump and very aromatic and are best used within two years of harvesting. Beyond that, they shrink and shrivel as the essential oils dry out. Clove oil is used in dental emergencies as it dulls the pain of toothaches. Store away from heat and light.

Coriander (Dhania)

Of all the Indian spices, coriander is one of two most widely used. A seed about the size of a peppercorn, golden brown in color, it is a versatile spice with a sweet, perfume-like aroma and a distinctive, sweetish taste. It is used in three forms in Indian cooking: the seed, whole or crushed; the seed, roasted and powdered, which makes it pleasantly nutty; and the leaves, referred to as fresh coriander, Chinese parsley or cilantro (see page 18). The leaves and seeds are not interchangeable as they have very different properties. Coriander is used in meat, seafood, vegetable and lentil dishes. Coriander seeds can be stored indefinitely in the pantry. Since ground spices deteriorate rapidly with exposure to air, roast and grind just enough to last six to eight weeks.

Cumin (Jeera)

Cumin, along with coriander, shares the distinction of being widely used throughout the country. It is a grayish, slightly thick seed about $\frac{1}{8}$ inch (0.25 cm) long, often referred to as "white" cumin. This is to distinguish it from the "black" cumin, called shah (royal) jeera.

The latter is finer and more delicate and is very expensive. It is used sparingly in rice dishes and a few north Indian meat preparations. Cumin seeds are used whole, usually flash-fried in hot oil, or toasted and powdered. Toasting releases the essential oils in the seeds, making them highly aromatic and mellow. Cumin is an aid to digestion. The seeds have an indefinite shelf life.

Fennel (Saunf)

Fennel seeds resemble white cumin seeds but are slightly larger and greenish yellow, with a flavor that is more like anise. They are usually used crushed or powdered in cooked dishes but are toasted when they are offered at the end of a meal as a mouth freshener and digestive aid.

In Indian restaurants, they are often placed in a dish mixed with small pieces of rock sugar for diners to take as they leave. An infusion of fennel seeds in boiling water is a well-known remedy for an upset stomach. Fennel seeds can be stored indefinitely.

Fenugreek (Methi)

Fenugreek seeds and leaves are very important in Indian cooking. The seeds are small, flat sided and bean-like, yellowish brown and very bitter. The leaves are also bitter but have a very different flavor; the two are not interchangeable. The seeds are used whole, at the beginning of a dish, when they are flash-fried, or powdered and used in pickles and spice blends. Fenugreek seeds are an important ingredient in sambar powder, the seasoning mix of south India. They are used in small quantities; about ½ tsp (2 mL) is usually sufficient to flavor a recipe for eight.

Mace (Javitri)

This is the orange-colored lacy outer covering of nutmeg, with a fragrance and taste similar to nutmeg, only milder.

Mango Powder (Amchur)

Unripe green mango is peeled, sliced and sun-dried before being powdered. The powder is grayish, mildly scented and sour. It is used in place of lemon juice in dry vegetable dishes and is always folded in at the end of cooking. It is bought pre-packaged and, unlike most other powdered spices, has an indefinite shelf life when stored in an airtight container in the refrigerator. It is an important ingredient in north Indian chaat (street food) dishes.

Mustard (Rai)

Dark mustard seeds are used throughout the country and are the primary seasoning in the food of the south and the eastern state of Bengal. Mustard greens (sarson) are a popular winter dish in the Punjab, where they are teamed with a griddle-baked corn bread.

The seeds are reddish brown but are commonly called black. Used whole, they are flash-fried in very hot oil until they pop. Popping is essential to release flavor and taste. Just adding the seeds to a boiling pot will do nothing for the dish. The seeds are also crushed and added to pickles, and when added to a brine-based pickle, they are a souring agent. Mustard seeds should be stored in a cool, dark place; they will remain fresh for up to two years.

Mustard oil is cold pressed from dark mustard seeds and has a strong flavor. It is not made from an infusion. It is used as the primary oil in Indian pickles and is also the preferred cooking oil in Bengal. It has medicinal uses as well; it is even warmed and used topically to relieve joint pain.

Nigella (Kalaunji)

Nigella, often mistakenly called onion seed, is a small, intensely black seed that is not actually onion seed at all! It only resembles it — hence the misleading name. It is flash-fried in hot oil to release its aroma and has a pleasant, distinctive taste. Nigella is used mainly in north Indian vegetable recipes and is also sprinkled on top of breads. It is always used whole. It is an important pickling spice and is part of the Bengali five-spice blend known as panch phoran (see page 18). Nigella seeds do not deteriorate with extended storage.

Nutmeg (Jaiphul)

Nutmeg is a gray-brown nut about ¾ to 1 inch (2 to 2.5 cm) in size and is enclosed in a hard, lacy covering called mace (javitri). It has a distinctive sweetish aroma and taste when powdered and is used mainly in north Indian dishes. It is best to buy whole nuts and freshly grate them as needed; nutmeg loses its aroma rather quickly when exposed to air. Store nutmeg, in an airtight container, for two to three years.

Pomegranate (Anardana)

The seeds of the bright red pomegranate are dark and about $\frac{1}{4}$ inch (0.5 cm) long when semi-dried. These are used whole, crushed, or roasted and powdered in dishes from the north, imparting a blackish color and sour taste. They are sold in small packages, often in the refrigerated section of Indian stores. Reddish seeds that are plump are an indication of freshness. Store package in a resealable freezer bag in the refrigerator for up to one year.

Poppy Seed (Khus-khus)

Indian poppy seeds are tiny, creamy white and without any aroma. They are added to spice blends or ground up in curry pastes to act as thickeners. Their use is more prevalent in north India and in Bengal, where they are an important ingredient and, in certain dishes, the primary seasoning, providing a distinctive taste and texture. Toasting poppy seeds before grinding into a paste enhances their nutty flavor. Store in an airtight container in the refrigerator for up to one year.

Red Chili (Lal Mirch)

Red chilies are a broad category in the world of Indian spices, and one of the most important. Red chilies are usually used in their dry form, and the potency varies with the variety. Some are used for their heat and can be searing. Others are used for their flavor and color, without the searing quality. Some have both. For the recipes in this book, I have used cayenne where I would use hot red chili powder, and paprika where I was looking for color without the heat. Peppers, both red and green, are what give Indian food its piquancy; simply reduce or eliminate to make the cuisine acceptable for people who cannot tolerate hot food. Most Indians develop not only a tolerance but also a craving for heat, and some even travel with their own supply of the hot stuff.

Saffron (Kesar)

Saffron, called the king of spices, is also the world's most expensive one. It is cultivated in Spain and Iran, and in Kashmir, India. It is the stigma of the crocus flower and is still harvested by hand. It takes more than 60,000 blooms to yield 1 lb (500 g) of saffron; hence the prohibitive cost. Saffron is sold as threads and as powder. I recommend using only the threads, as that is the purest form of saffron. The darker the threads, the better the quality.

To use saffron, it is best to soak it in a little hot water or hot milk before adding to the dish. Saffron has a delicate aroma and imparts a beautiful color to rice pulaos, desserts and sweets. It is also used in meat preparations in north India. It has a two-year shelf life and is best purchased at a reputable store that does a good business in spices, as that will ensure turnaround and, therefore, freshness.

Salt (Namak)

I prefer to use kosher salt, but any table salt is just as good. I believe salt is a matter of personal taste, so I hesitate to specify exact amounts.

Black salt (kala namak) is sulfuric and is an important flavor enhancer in north Indian street/snack foods (chaat). It is pinkish brown and has a strong, almost offensive odor. However, it has a pleasant taste and certainly adds oomph to the chaat dishes of the north, and to certain chutneys and relishes.

Sesame (Til, Gingelly)

White sesame seeds are used throughout the country, both toasted and untoasted, as whole seeds and also ground into a paste. The taste and flavor of sesame is nutty and distinctive, and the seeds provide a pleasant crunch. Sesame seed sweets are popular at festival times and are also used in Hindu temple rituals. Refrigerate sesame seeds in an airtight container for up to two years.

Sesame oil is used as a cooking medium and is also used to make Indian pickles.

Tamarind (Imli)

The tamarind tree is indigenous to India and is a large shade tree that lines the ancient travel routes in the south. The pod is knobby and flattish, about 4 to 5 inches (10 to 12.5 cm) long and tan colored. When the pod is ripe, the papery outer skin splits, revealing a soft, dark brown pulp on the inside that covers four or five large shiny brown seeds. The pods are processed commercially; the outer skin and seeds are removed and the flesh compressed into a brick about 8 inches (20 cm) long and 4 inches (10 cm) wide. It is very sour and is an important flavoring agent in lentil (dal) and seafood dishes, chutneys and relishes. To use tamarind brick, break off the specified amount from the brick and break into small pieces. Soak in hot water for 20 minutes to soften. Soften pods further with fingers and pour into a large-holed sieve set over a bowl. Strain, pressing down to push through as much of the thick pulp as possible. Discard the residual fibrous material remaining in the strainer.

There are several brands of tamarind pulp and concentrate on the market. I like the Thai tamarind pulp best as it is ready to use and similar to the tamarind pulp made from the brick. If unable to find this, Indian tamarind concentrate will do, but the dark color tends to alter the color of the dish. Store the brick tightly covered in the pantry; the prepared pulp and concentrate should be refrigerated after opening.

Turmeric (Haldi)

Turmeric, which gives Indian food its characteristic yellow color, is the rhizome of a plant of the ginger family, which is indigenous to India. Turmeric is bought and used in powder form as the root is too woody to be powdered in the home kitchen. The rule with turmeric is that a little goes a long way. When doubling a recipe, I suggest that you do not double the turmeric, just increase by half again. Too much turmeric in a dish will result in a bitter aftertaste.

Turmeric is used throughout the country in meat, seafood, vegetable and lentil preparations. It is used in Hindu religious and social rituals and also as a vegetable dye. It has antiseptic properties and is considered to be a blood purifier. It is used in making beauty products and also for tinting butter and prepared mustard. Be careful when using as turmeric stains are very difficult to remove. This spice can be stored indefinitely in the pantry in an airtight container.

Spice Blends

Chaat Masala

This quintessential north Indian mixture is salty and sour and is sprinkled on snacks and street foods. It's particularly popular in Delhi and Mumbai (Bombay). The main ingredient is black salt, the sulfuric salt previously mentioned. This is mixed with mango powder (amchur) or ground pomegranate seeds (anardana), powdered cumin and a little cayenne. As always, there are variations, but the main flavor profile remains the same. It is usually store-bought, and there are several good brands available.

Store the package in a resealable plastic freezer bag in the refrigerator. This is a delicious blend to sprinkle on salads, fish, french fries and baked potatoes.

Garam Masala

The most recognized Indian spice blend is no doubt garam masala, literally "warm mixture." A blend of aromatic spices, the basic recipe varies slightly as it is customized by individual families. It is a north Indian mixture and not used in south Indian dishes. There are several good brands on the market, but avoid buying spices from bulk bins as exposure to air causes them to deteriorate.

For approximately ¼ cup (50 mL) garam masala:
2 tbsp (25 mL) coriander seeds, toasted in a dry skillet (see Tips, page 74)
1 tbsp (15 mL) cumin seeds, toasted in a dry skillet (see Tips, page 73)
1 tsp (5 mL) peppercorns
3 sticks cinnamon (each 3 inches/7.5 cm long)
35 green cardamom pods
35 cloves
Combine all ingredients and grind in a coffee mill. Store in an airtight container.

Panch Phoran

This spice mix from Bengal is unique as it combines five very distinctive seeds. Literally translated, panch phoran means "five seeds." It is one of my favorite seasonings for a variety of vegetables. The mix can be stored in an airtight container for a year or two. Mix together equal quantities of dark mustard seeds, cumin seeds, fenugreek seeds, fennel and nigella. This mix is always flash-fried in a little oil before adding the main ingredients.

Sambar Powder

Sambar powder is a south Indian blend used extensively in southern food. A laundry list of ingredients includes fenugreek, peppercorns, red chilies, coriander, cumin, mustard seeds, turmeric, curry leaves and asafetida, among others. There are several good brands on the market that will remain fresh for one year if stored tightly closed and refrigerated.

Herbs

Cilantro (Hara dhania)

In India, cilantro, also known as fresh coriander or Chinese parsley, holds pride of place. Indian food without cilantro is unthinkable. The delicate, lacy leaves are used during cooking and as a garnish, and correct handling is important. I like to keep my cilantro in a bowl of water while cooking, to keep the leaves from wilting, and just before using I shake off excess water and chop coarsely before adding to the dish. Fine chopping results in discoloration as the cilantro oxidizes and turns blackish and has an offensive odor. Cilantro is the main ingredient in the famous fresh "green chutney," the ubiquitous dipping sauce served in Indian restaurants. To keep cilantro fresh, spread on a paper towel and remove any rotting matter. Cover with a second paper towel and set aside for one hour. Roll up both towels together, jellyroll fashion, and store in a plastic bag in refrigerator. Stored this way, cilantro will remain fresh for more than a week. Cilantro grows from coriander seeds; the two are not interchangeable.

Curry Leaves (Kari patta)

Curry leaves, also known as kari leaves, are much prized in Indian dishes, particularly in south India, for their unmistakable fragrance and flavor. Multiple-leaved citrus-smelling sprigs grow on a tree that can reach 15 feet, but they also thrive as potted plants in a sunny location. It is not to be confused with the feathery gray-green herbaceous plant that is known as curry plant and has a faint aroma of "curry." Fresh leaves are readily available in Indian markets. They should be refrigerated but will dry when kept for several weeks; however, they still retain their aroma. I prefer not to use the dried leaves available in packages from India; they lack aroma. If fresh leaves are unavailable, omit from recipe. There is no substitute.

Fresh Dill (Sua)

Used as a herb and also as a green, when mixed greens are called for, dill is used freely with vegetables and lentils.

Fresh Fenugreek (Methi)

After cilantro, fresh fenugreek leaves are the most utilized herb. The gray-green three-part leaves have a distinctive bitter flavor and are used in breads, with vegetables and also with meat and fish. The plant is used in Ayurvedic medicine, the ancient art of Indian herbal medicine, and is surprisingly good when dried. Dried fenugreek leaves, known as kasoori methi, are available in packages and should be stored in resealable plastic bags in the refrigerator for up to one year. Fenugreek seeds and leaves have very different tastes and are not interchangeable.

HINTS AND TIPS

Leftovers are a fact of life. How you handle them can turn you into a kitchen wizard or relegate you to the category of practical but boring. Food, for me, is a source of joy and an opportunity to be creative, rather than a chore that cannot be avoided. I would like to share my ideas so you, too, can have as much fun in the kitchen and, at the same time, become a hero to your family and friends.

Indians are by nature and necessity frugal. Nothing, in particular something as sacred as food, is wasted. Every morsel of food, cooked or otherwise, is made use of. Even peels, such as banana and squash, are turned into chutney! Leftovers, no matter how much or how little, are used in myriad ways. Leftover vegetables are coarsely mashed and mixed with a binding agent, such as boiled and mashed potato or dampened slices of bread, and pan-fried as patties. Pieces of boneless cooked meat or chicken are shredded and stir-fried with onions, tomatoes and sliced bell pepper, seasoned with a good dose of ginger, garlic and as many green chilies as the tongue can bear. A popular dish in Bombay kitchens, it is known as chili fry.

One of my favorite tricks is cooking twice as much rice as I need for a meal. Cooking time will not change, and you have a versatile staple to transform into a new dish a day or two later. Cooked rice reheats with great success in a microwave. It can also be turned into a stir-fried dish or a layered one-dish meal. If you have a leftover curry that is on the dry side, it can be layered with the cooked rice. Accompanied with raita, it becomes a quick and delicious meal. When the two components — rice and curry — are layered in this manner, the sum of the components goes far beyond the boring rice with leftovers. When the "new" dish is heated, the flavors combine, resulting in a far more complex-tasting dish and a new taste experience.

Leftover dals can be handled in various ways. They can be served as soup by adding a little water, fresh seasonings and herbs. Alternatively, leftover dal can be reduced over low heat to a thick paste and used as a filling for stuffed breads and vegetables.

Enjoy learning about Indian spices and flavors and then let your creativity soar as you incorporate these into your everyday cooking.

BASIC TECHNIQUES

The few simple techniques used in Indian cooking are easy to grasp. Understanding them will ensure success. Here's one basic tip to start: while stirring, cooking and browning food, scrape down the sides of the pan often to keep food from sticking. This prevents burnt food bits from falling into the pan. I find heatproof silicone spatulas work best.

Braising

This technique is one of the most important to understand and master. In Indian cooking, meat and poultry are sometimes marinated in a mixture of spices and seasonings, often moistened with yogurt or sometimes vinegar or lemon juice. The marinade then forms part of the finished dish and is incorporated into the sauce or gravy. The other ingredients of the gravy, such as onions, tomatoes, and so on, are sautéed and the meat or poultry added to the pan to brown. Then the marinade is added and the dish is simmered or braised, as specified in the recipe, to allow the meat to cook, the gravy to thicken and the flavors to combine. The correct pan size and cooking temperature are also important factors as they will affect the texture of the meat and the gravy in the finished dish.

Browning (Bhuno)

This is an important technique and crucial for achieving the desired flavor and appearance. Adequate browning of onions is particularly important in certain north Indian meat and poultry dishes; in many cases, the recipe calls for dark brown, almost blackened, onions. When combined with spices and other ingredients, the resulting gravy is rich and appealing. Browning of meats for certain curries is also important. I have developed a technique to brown onions in minimal oil, usually about 2 tbsp (25 mL) for eight servings, instead of the usual ½ cup (125 mL) in traditional cooking. Although this method requires a little more effort, the result is healthier because less oil is used without comprising flavor. When browning onions, it is best to coat them in hot oil and spread them in a single layer in the pan. To start out, maintain a medium-high heat to allow the inherent moisture in the onions to evaporate. Turn the onions every two minutes, spreading them in bottom of pan to cook evenly. As they begin to color, reduce heat and continue browning, maintaining an audible sizzle at all times to indicate the onions are cooking. At this stage, the browning is a result of caramelizing of the natural sugars. A slow process, it is the key to a successful mouth-watering gravy.

Deep-Frying

Indians love deep-fried foods. They are easy to whip up in a hurry, and vegetarian snacks, such as fritters (bhajias and pakoras), patties and assorted balls, are made with

COAST
hotels

refreshingly local

Grand Bahia Principe
cay cog

Dec, 18

165°C = 325°F

Cumin seeds
Cumin powder
coriander powder
chilli powder

Scott
Dephesus

0775-5330

simple ingredients that are staples in every Indian kitchen. Puffy steam-filled whole wheat breads (puris) are a favorite around the country; they are used to scoop up morsels and are a must on picnics and train journeys. And, of course, there are the famous papadums served in Indian restaurants in North America, often with brown and green dipping sauces. There are a few simple rules for successful deep-frying. Use a wok or electric skillet and add 2 to 3 inches (5 to 7.5 cm) of vegetable oil so that the food does not touch the bottom of the pan. It is important to maintain a steady temperature, which is why an electric skillet or wok is ideal. For best results, cook food in batches, without crowding, and do not stir. Allow two to three minutes of cooking (in most cases), then turn each piece to finish cooking according to directions. Avoid removing and adding individual pieces one at a time. Use a wire-mesh strainer or large-holed scoop to remove as many pieces as possible at one time and shake gently over pan to allow oil to drip before draining on paper towels. Do not use a slotted spoon as it does not drain adequately, resulting in greasy food.

Steam cooking (Dum)

Dum (steam) cooking is a versatile technique that has more than one meaning. The term is often used to describe the last few minutes of rice cooking, when the rice has absorbed all liquid but needs to firm up before serving. Once the rice is cooked, reduce the heat to as low as possible and let stand, undisturbed, for several minutes. This allows the starch in the rice to firm up and form a protective coating on each grain, so the grains remain separate and do not become gummy.

The technique is particularly important in vegetable dishes, allowing one to cook wholesome, nutritious dishes without the addition of liquid. After sautéing vegetables in the seasoned oil, add a spoonful or two of water to help start the condensation process. Cover with a tight-fitting lid to retain the condensed moisture in the pan and prevent evaporation. Stir periodically to ensure even cooking and to prevent burning. The finished dish is not only full of flavor and complexity, but also highly nutritious. This method of cooking foods in their inherent moisture is called cooking on "dum" or by using the trapped steam.

Tempering (Tadka or Baghar)

The instant flash-frying of whole spices and seeds in a small amount of very hot oil is an essential step in the cooking of every region of the country. When seeds and spices are tossed into very hot oil, within seconds they release their volatile oils and essences. This does not occur when they are just stirred into a dish while cooking. In the case of meat, vegetable and rice dishes, the flash-frying is usually done at the beginning of the dish. Lentils, on the other hand, are often boiled until soft, then the flash-fried seasonings are added.

Toasting and grinding spices

Toasting spices releases their essential oils and intensifies their flavors. Toasting changes the flavor and aroma of spices such as coriander and cumin; when either of these seeds is toasted then ground, the resulting taste is completely different than when ground without toasting. Whereas whole spices have an almost indefinite shelf life, powdered spices are fragile, and with exposure to air they will lose their freshness and fragrance over a period of time. I suggest you toast and grind small quantities so that you use them within eight to ten weeks.

Heat a dry heavy skillet on medium heat for two to three minutes. Place whole spices, such as coriander or cumin seeds in a single layer in the pan. Shake pan periodically to brown seeds evenly. Within three to four minutes, the spices will begin to turn darker and release their aroma. Stir for a few more seconds and transfer to a bowl to cool. Grind in a coffee grinder reserved for spices. Store in an airtight jar away from heat.

Handling a fresh coconut

Thanks to the popularity of Thai food, grated frozen coconut and canned coconut milk are now easy to obtain. However, should you wish to obtain the grated meat from a whole coconut, here is what to do. Buy a coconut that is heavy and has plenty of liquid sloshing around inside. If it appears light and dry, it is too old and dried out, and chances are the meat will be rancid. Make sure there is no oozing of liquid near the three eyes of the fruit. Place the coconut on a hard surface near the sink and tap it smartly with a hammer. If you crack it open with a single stroke, the liquid inside can be saved and used as a drink. With an old knife (be sure not to use one of your best ones as it can be damaged), pry the meat loose from the hard brown shell. Next, using a vegetable peeler, remove the brown skin from the meat. The white meat can either be frozen in freezer bags or grated in the food processor and then frozen for up to nine months.

To make coconut milk

Place grated coconut in a bowl. Pour twice as much hot water over top and set aside for 30 minutes. Strain through cheesecloth, twisting to obtain as much liquid as possible. Discard spent coconut.

To make crisp fried onions (birishta)

Shreds of crisp fried onion are available in Indian stores in packages or plastic jars, in several sizes. A versatile ingredient, fried onion is added to marinades and curries, and used as a garnish on pulaos (pilafs). Surprisingly, store-bought fried onions remain crisp and retain freshness for up to one year when refrigerated after opening. To make your own fried onions, heat oil for deep-frying in a wok or skillet on medium-high. Add thinly sliced onions to cover entire surface. Let stand, without stirring, for five minutes. As edges begin to brown, move the browned onions to the middle of the wok, moving uncooked onions to the edges. Continue to cook with minimal stirring until onions are evenly browned. Remove with wire-mesh strainer, draining well, and spread in single layer on paper towels. Let cool completely. Fried onions can be refrigerated in resealable plastic bag for up to four months.

Frying nuts and dried fruit

Fried nuts and raisins are often used in desserts and as garnishes on pulaos and other dishes. In a skillet, heat oil over medium and stir in nuts and raisins. Cook, stirring continuously, until nuts are golden and raisins are puffy, about two minutes. Drain and transfer to paper towels.

Snacks and Appetizers

INDIANS ARE ENTHUSIASTIC snackers. Tikkis (patties), pakoras (fritters), all kinds of store-bought fried snacks, spicy nuts and wafers (potato chips) are consumed with gusto.

Entertaining at home is an Indian tradition, and weekends are for meeting with friends at someone's home. Children and young adults are always included in these gatherings, and plentiful snacks are provided to fill in the hour or two before the meal is served.

In addition, Indians love eating small plates of snacks called "chaat," available from street vendors and small corner eating places. These chaat shops are often no bigger than a hole in the wall, with room only for the owner-cook and the tiniest of spaces for cooking (it cannot really be called a kitchen, but it functions as one), from which he turns out the most amazing, mouth-watering concoctions. These are always vegetarian and consist of several ingredients, like diced boiled potatoes, feathery puffed rice, hair-thin bits of chickpea flour fried noodles, chopped onions, cilantro, green chilies and puris (small crispy crackers) — all tossed together with a couple of large spoonfuls of assorted chutneys that are like dipping sauces. I have wonderful memories of making frequent detours walking home with my friends after school to share snacks and conversation at a popular chaat shop, which has now, more than 50 years later, morphed into a large eat-in restaurant doing great business. In fact, it now has a very successful mail-order business and even ships to North America.

In this chapter, I have included recipes for popular but simple finger foods that are typically served at home, alongside bowls of crispy snacks available in Indian stores.

* * *

Aloo Chaat
Spicy Boiled Potatoes

Serves 4 to 6		

I love to make these potatoes as an accompaniment to barbecued or grilled meats because their wonderful texture contrasts nicely with the grilled flavors. In summer, they make a tasty light lunch, especially when made with buttery gold potatoes.

❋

1 lb	potatoes (about 3)	500 g
1 tbsp	cumin powder	15 mL
1/2 tsp	coriander powder	2 mL
1/2 tsp	mango powder (amchur) or 1 tbsp (15 mL) freshly squeezed lemon juice	2 mL
1/4 tsp	cayenne pepper	1 mL
1 tsp	salt or to taste	5 mL
1	lime or lemon	1
2 to 3 tbsp	cilantro, chopped	25 to 45 mL

1. In a saucepan of boiling water, cook whole potatoes with skins on until tender, 20 to 25 minutes. Drain. When cool enough to handle, peel and cut into 1/4-inch (0.5 cm) thick slices. Set aside.

2. In a small bowl, combine cumin, coriander, mango powder, cayenne pepper and salt.

3. Arrange potatoes, slightly overlapping, on a serving platter. Sprinkle with spice mixture. (Can be tented with foil and set aside at room temperature for up to 4 hours.)

4. Just before serving, squeeze lime juice over potatoes and sprinkle with cilantro.

Bataka Nu Rotla

Crustless Potato Pie

A friend who was visiting from Bombay gave me this recipe when I said that the house rule for all guests was to provide a recipe per day of stay. We prepared the dish just before dashing off to the airport, and it wasn't until later that I discovered what a winner it was.

❋

TIP

The pie can be made earlier in the day and served at room temperature. It's good picnic fare as well.

◆ *Preheat oven to 400°F (200°C)*
◆ *9-inch (23 cm) pie plate, sprayed with vegetable spray*

2 lbs	all-purpose potatoes (about 6)	1 kg
1/3 cup	raw cashews	75 mL
1/3 cup	raisins	75 mL
2 tbsp	chickpea flour (besan)	25 mL
1 tsp	granulated sugar	5 mL
1 tsp	cayenne pepper	5 mL
1/2 tsp	turmeric	2 mL
1/4 tsp	asafetida (hing)	1 mL
2	bay leaves, finely chopped	2
3/4 cup	cilantro, chopped	175 mL
1/4 cup	lime or lemon juice	50 mL
2 tsp	salt or to taste	10 mL
	Vegetable spray	

1. In a saucepan of boiling water, cook whole potatoes with skins on until tender, 20 to 25 minutes. Drain. When cool enough to handle, but still warm, peel and coarsely mash in a large bowl.

2. Boil cashews and raisins in 1 cup (250 mL) water for 5 minutes. Drain and add to potatoes.

3. In a small bowl, stir together chickpea flour, sugar, cayenne pepper, turmeric, asafetida and bay leaves. Sprinkle over potatoes. Scatter cilantro on top. Drizzle with lemon juice and sprinkle with salt. Mix thoroughly by hand.

4. Pat mixture into prepared dish. Smooth top. Mist with vegetable spray. Bake in preheated oven until golden, 35 to 40 minutes. Let cool for 10 minutes and cut into wedges. Serve with chutney of your choice.

Dhokla

Steamed Semolina Squares

Serves 8

These fluffy, light appetizers have almost become my signature dish. This adapted recipe came to me via a young Indian friend whose family settled in East Africa several decades ago. The original recipe is from the state of Gujerat — known for its excellent vegetarian offerings — but it takes two days to prepare. This version takes only 30 minutes, and not even the most die-hard purist has been able to tell the difference.

Tips

Refrigerate leftovers in an airtight container. Warm in microwave to restore freshness.

Eno fruit salts are a digestive aid and are used in this recipe to aerate the batter while steaming, in lieu of the fermentation that helps to lighten the batter in the traditional recipe. They are available in Indian grocery stores.

- *Steamer with very hot water*
- *9-inch (2.5 L) square cake pan, sprayed with vegetable spray*

1 cup	quick-cooking cream of wheat	250 mL
1 cup	plain nonfat yogurt	250 mL
1/4 cup	lemon juice	50 mL
2 tbsp	chickpea flour (besan)	25 mL
1 tsp	minced green chilies, preferably serranos	5 mL
1 tsp	grated peeled gingerroot	5 mL
1 tsp	salt	5 mL
1/2 tsp	granulated sugar	2 mL
1/4 tsp	turmeric	1 mL
2 1/2 tbsp	vegetable oil, divided	32 mL
1 tsp	Eno fruit salts (see Tips, left)	5 mL
1 tsp	mustard seeds	5 mL
2 tbsp	cilantro, chopped	25 mL

1. In a mixing bowl, stir together cream of wheat, yogurt, 1/2 cup (125 mL) lukewarm water, lemon juice, chickpea flour, chilies, ginger, salt, sugar and turmeric.
2. In a saucepan, heat 1 1/2 tbsp (22 mL) of the oil until very hot. Pour into mixture and stir well.
3. When ready to steam, stir Eno fruit salts into cream of wheat mixture and pour into prepared pan. Place pan in steamer and steam until top springs back when touched, 12 to 15 minutes. Let cool slightly.
4. In a small saucepan, heat remaining oil over medium heat until very hot. Add mustard seeds and cover immediately. When seeds stop popping in a few seconds, pour over mixture. Sprinkle with cilantro. Cut into 1 1/2-inch (4 cm) squares or diamond shapes and serve with chutney of your choice.

Corn Bhel
Corn and Potato Toss

This type of dish is typically served at informal gatherings and, until recently, was never part of a formal meal. It is representative of the street foods of north India and the area around Mumbai (formerly known as Bombay), India's equivalent of New York City. This dish has since been elevated to appetizer status and is now sometimes served in dainty portions at elegant dinner parties.

❋

TIPS

Sev is a vermicelli-type snack made from chickpea flour (besan). It comes ready to eat and should not be confused with the vermicelli used for making a type of dessert. It is available in Indian stores.

◆

You can buy cilantro chutney in Indian stores if you do not care to make your own.

CILANTRO CHUTNEY

2 cups	cilantro leaves and soft stems	500 mL
3 to 4	green chilies, preferably serranos	3 to 4
1 tsp	chopped peeled gingerroot	5 mL
1 tsp	granulated sugar	5 mL
1/4 cup	lemon juice	50 mL
1/4 tsp	salt or to taste	1 mL

CORN AND POTATO MIX

2 cups	cooked corn	500 mL
2 cups	diced boiled potatoes	500 mL
1/2 cup	cilantro, chopped	125 mL
1/3 cup	diced red onion	75 mL
1 1/2 tsp	cumin powder	7 mL
1/2 tsp	cayenne pepper	2 mL
1 tsp	salt	5 mL
1/4 cup	lime juice	50 mL
3/4 cup	sev (see Tips, left)	175 mL
2	chapatis or tortillas, baked until crisp, broken into small pieces	2
2 tbsp	cilantro, chopped, for garnish	25 mL

1. *Cilantro Chutney:* In a blender, combine cilantro, chilies, ginger, sugar, lemon juice, 1/2 cup (125 mL) water and salt. Combine 1/4 cup (50 mL) of the chutney with 1/3 cup (75 mL) water. (Refrigerate the rest in an airtight container for up to 1 month.)

2. *Corn and Potato Mix:* In a large bowl, stir together corn, potatoes, cilantro, onion, cumin, cayenne pepper and salt. Stir in lime juice and chutney.

3. When ready to serve, gently mix in sev and chapati pieces. Mound on a platter. Garnish with cilantro and serve immediately.

Mung Dal ki Tikki
Yellow Mung Bean Patties

Versatile and make-ahead appetizers such as these are perfect for a party. They can be refrigerated for a day in an airtight container and reheated in a 250°F (120°C) oven for 10 minutes.

2 cups	yellow mung beans (yellow mung dal)	500 mL
2 cups	finely chopped cabbage	500 mL
2 to 3 tsp	minced green chilies, preferably serranos	10 to 15 mL
1 1/2 tbsp	chickpea flour (besan)	22 mL
1/2 tsp	baking soda	2 mL
1/4 tsp	asafetida (hing)	1 mL
2 tbsp	lime or lemon juice	25 mL
3 tbsp	cilantro, chopped	45 mL
2 tsp	salt or to taste	10 mL
3 to 4 tbsp	vegetable oil, divided	45 to 60 mL

1. Clean and pick through beans for any small stones and grit. Rinse several times in cold water until water is fairly clear. Soak in 3 to 4 inches (7.5 to 10 cm) water for at least 4 hours or until softened, or for up to 8 hours.

2. Drain, rinse and drain again. Grind coarsely in food processor. Transfer to a bowl.

3. Stir in cabbage, chilies, chickpea flour, baking soda, asafetida, lime juice, cilantro and salt. Mix well and chill for 30 minutes.

4. Heat a nonstick griddle or heavy nonstick skillet over medium heat and spread it with 1 tbsp (15 mL) of the oil. Divide mixture into 20 equal portions. If mixture is slightly runny, mix in 1 to 2 tbsp (15 to 25 mL) chickpea flour, just enough to make soft patties. Form each portion into a disc about 1/2 inch (1 cm) thick. Cook patties, 4 at a time, on hot griddle until brown, 1 1/2 to 2 minutes per side. Repeat with remaining patties and oil in batches, heating oil and griddle in between batches. Serve with chutney of your choice.

Aloo aur Keema ki Tikki

Meat and Potato Patties

Allspice is grown in Kashmir and used sparingly in a few north Indian dishes. Its distinctive flavor and aroma add a new twist to this favorite dish.

TIP

Patties such as these are often served as street food, sandwiched between 2 slices of white bread and accompanied by marinated onion rings or chutney.

1 lb	all-purpose potatoes (about 3)	500 g
1 lb	lean ground beef or ground lamb	500 g
1 1/2 tsp	powdered allspice	7 mL
3/4 tsp	turmeric	4 mL
3/4 tsp	cayenne pepper	4 mL
1 1/4 cups	very finely minced red onion (about 1 large)	300 mL
1/2 cup	cilantro, chopped	125 mL
1/2 cup	fresh mint, finely chopped, or 1 tbsp (15 mL) dried mint	125 mL
2 tsp	grated peeled gingerroot	10 mL
2 tsp	garlic paste or very finely minced garlic	10 mL
2 tbsp	lemon juice	25 mL
2 tsp	salt or to taste	10 mL
3/4 cup	dry bread crumbs	175 mL
1 cup	vegetable oil	250 mL

1. In a saucepan of boiling water, cook whole potatoes with skins on until tender, 20 to 25 minutes. Drain. When cool enough to handle, peel and mash. Set aside.

2. In a skillet over medium heat, sauté ground meat, breaking up any lumps, until no longer pink, 4 to 5 minutes. Let cool to room temperature.

3. Combine meat with potatoes, allspice, turmeric, cayenne pepper, onion, cilantro, mint, ginger, garlic, lemon juice and salt. Mix together by hand, kneading to a smooth dough. Adjust seasonings.

4. Divide mixture into 16 portions and form each portion into a patty about 1/2 inch (1 cm) thick, making sure sides are smooth and free of cracks. Dip in bread crumbs, pressing to coat.

5. Heat 2 tbsp (25 mL) of the oil in a skillet over medium heat. Add 3 to 4 patties and sauté, turning once, until golden on both sides, 3 to 4 minutes. Drain on paper towels. Repeat with remaining patties and oil in batches, heating oil and skillet in between batches. Serve hot with chutney of your choice.

Sheekh Kababs
Skewered Grilled Kababs

Makes 10 kababs

Sheekhs (metal skewers) are used extensively for cooking tandoori foods. It is best to use slightly flat metal skewers so foods do not rotate when being turned. Dampened bread is used as a binder and helps to keep the kababs soft.

❋

TIPS

For cocktail-size appetizers, cut each kabab into 4 pieces and serve with toothpicks. Kababs can be cooked up to 2 hours ahead, cooled, covered and refrigerated until ready to serve. To serve, wrap in foil and reheat in 350°F (180°C) oven for 10 minutes.

◆

Twice-ground meat makes softer, silkier kababs, an important feature of sheekh kababs. Ask your butcher to put the meat through the grinder a second time.

◆ *Preheat grill to medium-high*
◆ *10 flat metal skewers*

3	slices white bread	3
1 lb	ground lamb or beef sirloin, twice ground (see Tips, left)	500 g
20	blanched almonds, ground to powder in blender, or 3 tbsp (45 mL) almond meal	20
½ cup	minced onion	125 mL
2 tbsp	cilantro, chopped	25 mL
1 tbsp	minced peeled gingerroot	15 mL
1 tsp	minced garlic	5 mL
1 tsp	minced green chilies, preferably serranos	5 mL
2 tsp	coriander powder	10 mL
1 tsp	garam masala	5 mL
¾ tsp	cayenne pepper	4 mL
½ tsp	turmeric	2 mL
1½ tsp	salt or to taste	7 mL
1	egg	1
⅓ cup	vegetable oil	75 mL
1	onion, sliced into thin rounds and separated into rings, for garnish	1
	Lemon wedges for garnish	

1. Very quickly, dip bread, one slice at a time, into a bowl of water. Squeeze dry between palms and tear into pieces.

2. In a bowl, combine ground lamb, almonds, onion, cilantro, ginger, garlic, chilies, coriander, garam masala, cayenne pepper, turmeric, salt, egg and dampened bread. Thoroughly mix together by hand.

3. Divide mixture into 10 portions. Form each portion into a 6-inch (15 cm) long roll (kabab) around skewer. Brush with oil. Grill for 6 to 7 minutes, turning once, until no longer pink inside.

4. Garnish with onion rings and lemon wedges. Serve with chutney of your choice.

Chicken Boti Kababs

Saffron-Scented Chicken Kababs

Saffron adds a special touch to these succulent, bite-size pieces of chicken. They are delicious cooked on a charcoal grill.

TIP

It is not always necessary to thread kababs in Indian cooking. In this recipe, you can bake them without threading or grill them on skewers.

♦ *12 to 16 metal skewers, or 16 to 20 bamboo skewers, soaked in water for 30 minutes*

8	skinless boneless chicken breasts	8
½ tsp	saffron threads	2 mL
½ cup	plain nonfat yogurt, avoiding as much liquid as possible	125 mL
2 tbsp	minced green chilies, preferably serranos, or to taste	25 mL
1½ tbsp	minced peeled gingerroot	22 mL
1½ tbsp	minced garlic	22 mL
1½ tsp	cumin powder	7 mL
¾ tsp	cardamom powder	4 mL
½ tsp	freshly ground black pepper	2 mL
1½ tsp	salt or to taste	7 mL
3 tbsp	lemon or lime juice	45 mL
2 tbsp	vegetable oil (approx.)	25 mL

1. Rinse chicken and pat dry. Cut into bite-size pieces.

2. Soak saffron in 2 tbsp (25 mL) hot water for 10 minutes.

3. Stir together yogurt, chilies, ginger, garlic, cumin, cardamom, pepper, salt and lemon juice. Stir in saffron threads with liquid. Pour over chicken and mix thoroughly. Refrigerate for at least 2 hours or for up to 12 hours.

4. *To bake in oven:* Preheat oven to 375°F (190°C). Line a rimmed jelly-roll pan or baking sheet with foil. Arrange chicken pieces on pan, discarding extra marinade. Drizzle oil evenly on top. Bake until no longer pink inside, 10 to 12 minutes. Serve immediately.

5. *To cook on grill:* Preheat barbecue to medium. Thread chicken pieces onto metal skewers, 3 to 4 per skewer. If using bamboo skewers, wrap exposed bamboo with foil to prevent burning. Brush lightly with oil and grill, turning once, until no longer pink inside, 3 to 4 minutes.

Kande ka Bhajia
Onion Fritters

Serves 8

These onion clusters are light and crunchy, with just a hint of batter. Serve them hot or at room temperature — they're great with cocktails or to pack for a picnic.

TIPS

The secret to these ethereal nibbles is no water in the batter. Lightly rubbing the chickpea flour into the softened onion shreds, using the onion juices produced by salting and draining the excess onion moisture, is what makes these so crisp and crunchy.

♦

Fritters are best eaten when freshly made, but they can be made up to 3 hours ahead, loosely covered and stored at room temperature. Reheat at low temperature in the oven until crisp, 10 to 12 minutes.

- Deep-fryer or wok
- Candy/deep-fry thermometer

3	large onions	3
2 tsp	salt or to taste	10 mL
	Vegetable oil for deep-frying	
½ cup	chickpea flour (besan) (approx.)	125 mL
¼ tsp	cayenne pepper or more to taste	1 mL

1. Cut onions in half from tip to stem, then thinly slice with the grain. Place in a bowl. Sprinkle with salt and work it into onions with fingers. Set aside for 30 minutes to allow onions to sweat and soften.

2. Meanwhile, heat oil in deep-fryer to 375°F (190°C).

3. Drain off any onion juice that accumulates in bowl. Sprinkle ¼ cup (50 mL) of the chickpea flour over onions and rub lightly with fingers (see Tips, left). Continue adding chickpea flour by the tablespoon (15 mL) until onions begin to hold together in a clump.

4. Drop clumps into hot oil and fry in batches, without crowding, until crisp and golden, 4 to 5 minutes. Remove with slotted spoon and drain on paper towels. Serve hot with chutney of your choice.

Clockwise from top left: Batter-Dipped Vegetable Fritters (Vegetable Pakoras) (page 33), Onion Fritters (Kande ka Bhajia) (this page) and Tamarind Chutney (page 168)

Vegetable Pakoras
Batter-Dipped Vegetable Fritters

Pakoras, or bhajias as they are also called, are a favorite snack. There are numerous kinds of pakoras, this being one of the simplest and most popular. You can use a variety of vegetables, including cauliflower, sweet potato and even fresh spinach.

✳

TIP
These pakoras are best eaten as soon as they are cooked; they lose their crispness as they sit.

◆ *Deep-fryer or wok*
◆ *Candy/deep-fry thermometer*

2 cups	chickpea flour (besan)	500 mL
1 tsp	salt	5 mL
1/2 tsp	cayenne pepper	2 mL
1/2 tsp	baking soda	2 mL
8	eggplant slices, unpeeled, 1/4 inch (0.5 cm) thick	8
8	red or green bell pepper slices, 1/4 inch (0.5 cm) thick	8
8	zucchini slices, unpeeled, 1/4 inch (0.5 cm) thick	8
8	potato slices, peeled, 1/8 inch (0.25 cm) thick	8
	Vegetable oil for deep-frying	

1. In a bowl, mix together chickpea flour, salt, cayenne pepper and baking soda. Slowly pour in 1 cup (250 mL) water, stirring to a smooth consistency and adding up to 1/4 cup (50 mL) more water, a little at a time, until batter is slightly thinner than pancake batter. Set aside for 15 minutes.

2. Heat oil in deep-fryer to 375°F (190°C). One at a time, dip slices of eggplant, pepper, zucchini and potato into batter. Add to hot oil in batches of 5 or 6 and deep-fry until golden, 3 to 4 minutes. Remove with slotted spoon and drain on paper towels. Serve immediately with chutney of your choice.

Yellow Lentil Soup with Vegetables *(Toor Dal Soup with Vegetables)* (page 56)

Sindhi Pakoras
Sindhi Fritters

Serves 6 to 8

*These unusual fritters
from my own ethnic
background are perhaps
the only fritters that
can be frozen. Rainy
days always meant
gossip sessions over
cups of sweet hot
masala chai and
Sindhi pakoras.*

❋

TIP

Fritters can be made up
to 3 hours ahead. Serve
at room temperature or
reheat briefly in 250°F
(120°C) oven. You can
make ahead through
Step 3 and freeze in a
resealable plastic bag for
up to 2 months. Do not
thaw before proceeding
with recipe.

◆ *Deep-fryer or wok*
◆ *Candy/deep-fry thermometer*

1 cup	chickpea flour (besan)	250 mL
3 tbsp	cilantro, chopped	45 mL
1 tsp	minced green chilies, preferably serranos	5 mL
1 tbsp	pomegranate seeds (anardana), crushed	15 mL
1 tbsp	coriander seeds, crushed	15 mL
1 tsp	salt	5 mL
½ tsp	cayenne pepper	2 mL
1 cup	minced onion (about 1 large)	250 mL
⅔ cup	finely diced potato	150 mL
2 tbsp	finely diced tomato	25 mL
	Vegetable oil for deep-frying	

1. In a large bowl, combine chickpea flour, cilantro, chilies, crushed pomegranate and coriander seeds, salt and cayenne pepper. Blend in enough water (up to ¼ cup/50 mL), a little at a time, so dough holds together. (The mixture should be thick enough to drop by large spoonfuls to form dumpling-like shapes in hot oil.)

2. Stir in onion, potato and tomato.

3. Heat oil in deep-fryer to 350°F (180°C). Drop batter by heaping tablespoons (15 mL) into hot oil and fry in batches, without crowding, until pale golden, about 2 minutes. Remove with slotted spoon and drain on paper towels. Tear each pakora into 3 to 4 pieces with fingers.

4. Increase oil temperature to 400°F (200°C). Refry fritters in batches, without crowding, until crisp and edges are brown, about 1 minute. Remove with slotted spoon and drain on paper towels. Serve hot with chutney of your choice.

Rice, Cereal and Breads

G RAINS AND RICE occupy pride of place in the Indian diet. While brown rice is not commonly eaten, grains, on the other hand, are most often ground whole, as in chapati flour (atta), which is whole durum wheat milled very fine. Atta is what we use to make our daily griddle-baked flatbread, flaky parathas and the intriguing feather-light puffed puri. North Indian breads are world-famous. Arguably the best known is naan, which came to India with the Moghuls, who also introduced the enormous variety of rich layered and flavored breads, such as parathas, kulchas and batura.

Other flours used to make a variety of delicious and healthy breads include millet and sorghum, grown in the north, and ragi, grown in the southeast. These make wonderful peasant-type breads, full of flavor and rich in nutrients.

Those who live in the north eat more grains than rice, whereas in the south, where more than 20 varieties of rice are grown, the diet is based almost entirely on rice. Having said that, I need to qualify my statement. The famous elaborate biriyanis and pulaos, rich with lamb and perfumed with saffron, immediately come to mind when we think of Indian banquets; these are also a gift of the Moghuls, who influenced Indian life for three centuries. Their legacy changed forever the food of the north, known the world over for its refinement and richness.

Basmati rice is grown in the foothills of the Himalayan Mountains, where the soil, water and growing conditions give this rice its unique taste and aroma. It is not grown in other parts of the country.

I have chosen a cross-section of recipes that I think are versatile, easy to prepare and, most of all, very tasty.

❧   ❧   ❧

Perfect Steamed Rice

There are many ways to cook steamed rice. In some regions, a large pot of salted water is brought to a boil, then drained rinsed rice is stirred in and returned to a boil. After two minutes, the water is drained and the rice is covered and left on very low heat to finish steaming. I find the method I use here to be the simplest and healthiest because the minerals and vitamins are retained and absorbed into the water rather than lost when drained. Plus it's foolproof.

❋

TIP

Rice is always transferred to a serving platter, never a bowl, as the weight of the freshly steamed rice would cause the rice on the bottom to get mushy.

2 cups	Indian basmati rice	500 mL
1 tbsp	vegetable oil	15 mL
2 tsp	salt or to taste	10 mL

1. Place rice in a bowl with plenty of cold water and swish vigorously with fingers. Drain. Repeat process 4 or 5 times until water is fairly clear. Cover with 3 to 4 inches (7.5 to 10 cm) water and soak for at least 15 minutes or for up to 2 hours.

2. In a saucepan with a tight-fitting lid, heat oil over medium-high heat. Drain rice and add to saucepan. Stir to coat rice with oil. Add 3½ cups (825 mL) cold water and salt. Cover and bring to a boil over high heat. Reduce heat as low as possible and cook, covered, for 25 minutes, without peeking.

3. Remove from heat and set lid slightly ajar to allow steam to escape. Let rest for 5 minutes. Gently fluff with fork and carefully spoon onto platter to serve.

Peas Pulao
Spice-Scented Peas Pilaf

	Serves 8	

2 cups	Indian basmati rice	500 mL
2 tbsp	vegetable oil	25 mL
1	cinnamon stick, 2 inches (5 cm) long	1
6	whole cloves	6
2	bay leaves	2
1 cup	finely sliced onion (about 1)	250 mL
1 cup	frozen peas	250 mL
2 tsp	salt or to taste	10 mL

Pulao is synonymous with pilaf, and this is the simplest of the genre. It is also one of the most delicious — good not only with Indian dishes but equally compatible with non-Indian entrées. It is very quick and easy to prepare.

✳

TIP

The grains of rice are very fragile when they are just cooked. Gently spoon onto a platter, taking care not to break up the grains or else the rice will be mushy.

1. Place rice in a bowl with plenty of cold water and swish vigorously with fingers. Drain. Repeat process 4 or 5 times until water is fairly clear. Cover with 3 to 4 inches (7.5 to 10 cm) water and soak for at least 15 minutes or for up to 2 hours.

2. In a saucepan with a tight-fitting lid, heat oil over medium–high heat. Add cinnamon, cloves and bay leaves. Sauté until cloves puff up, about 1 minute. Add onion and sauté until golden brown, 6 to 8 minutes.

3. Drain rice and stir into onions. Add peas and mix well. Add 3½ cups (875 mL) cold water and salt. Cover and bring to a boil over high heat. Reduce heat to as low as possible and cook, covered, for 25 minutes, without peeking.

4. Remove from heat and set lid slightly ajar to allow steam to escape. Let rest for 5 minutes. Discard cinnamon stick, cloves and bay leaves, if desired. Gently fluff with fork and carefully spoon onto platter to serve.

Gobi Pulao
Basmati Rice with Spiced Cauliflower

Pulaos (pilafs) are wonderful one-dish meals. I love cauliflower, and this is one of my favorite dishes, especially when served with raita (yogurt salad) and a spicy store-bought pickle. Of course, it is just as good served with lamb or beef curry.

✳

TIP

You can complete Steps 2 and 3 several hours ahead. Reheat before adding rice.

2½ cups	Indian basmati rice	625 mL
3 tbsp	vegetable oil	45 mL
2½ cups	chopped onions	625 mL
1 tbsp	minced peeled gingerroot	15 mL
1 tbsp	minced garlic	15 mL
1 tbsp	Asian red chili paste (sambal olek)	15 mL
¾ tsp	black peppercorns	4 mL
6	whole cloves	6
2	bay leaves	2
4 cups	cauliflower florets	1 L
2 cups	chopped Roma tomatoes	500 mL
2 tsp	coriander powder	10 mL
1 tsp	cumin powder	5 mL
1 tsp	garam masala	5 mL
¾ tsp	turmeric	4 mL
2½ tsp	salt	12 mL

1. Place rice in a bowl with plenty of cold water and swish with fingers. Drain. Repeat process 4 or 5 times until water is fairly clear. Cover with 3 to 4 inches (7.5 to 10 cm) water and soak for at least 15 minutes or for up to 2 hours.

2. In a large saucepan with a tight-fitting lid, heat oil over medium-high heat. Stir in onions and sauté until dark brown, 12 to 15 minutes. Adjust heat as onions begin to color.

3. Add ginger, garlic, chili paste, peppercorns, cloves and bay leaves. Cook for 2 minutes. Add cauliflower and tomatoes. Cook for 2 minutes. Add coriander, cumin, garam masala, turmeric and salt. Mix well.

4. Drain rice and stir into vegetables. Pour in 4 cups (1 L) water. Cover and bring to a boil over high heat. Reduce heat as low as possible and cook, covered, for 25 minutes, without peeking.

5. Remove from heat and set lid slightly ajar to allow steam to escape. Let rest for 5 minutes. Discard peppercorns, cloves and bay leaves, if desired. Gently fluff with fork and carefully spoon onto platter to serve.

Pyaz ka Pulao
Caramelized Onion–Flavored Rice

This pulao was prepared in our home on special occasions, and I remember that in my grandmother's home it was the best. Almost blackened onions reduced to a sweet jam-like mass give the dish its dark brown color and astonishingly rich, sweet taste.

TIP

Garnish with quartered hard-cooked eggs, fried raisins and cashews (see Tip, page 43).

2 cups	Indian basmati rice	500 mL
3 tbsp	vegetable oil	45 mL
2	bay leaves	2
2	cinnamon sticks, each 2 inches (5 cm) long	2
6	whole cloves	6
3	large onions, sliced lengthwise	3
2½ tsp	salt or to taste	12 mL

1. Place rice in a bowl with plenty of cold water and swish with fingers. Drain. Repeat process 4 or 5 times until water is fairly clear. Cover with 3 to 4 inches (7.5 to 10 cm) water and soak for at least 15 minutes or for up to 2 hours.

2. In a large saucepan with a tight-fitting lid, heat oil over medium–high heat. Add bay leaves, cinnamon and cloves. Sauté until fragrant, about 1 minute.

3. Stir in onions. Sauté, stirring frequently, until almost caramelized, 20 to 25 minutes. Reduce heat as onions begin to color and continue to cook, adding a spoonful of water periodically to prevent burning.

4. When onions are dark brown and caramelized, drain rice and stir into pan. Mix well. Add 3½ cups (875 mL) water and salt. Cover and bring to a boil over high heat. Reduce heat to as low as possible and cook, covered, for 25 minutes, without peeking.

5. Remove from heat and set lid slightly ajar to allow steam to escape. Let rest for 5 minutes. Discard bay leaves, cinnamon sticks and cloves, if desired. Gently fluff with fork and carefully spoon onto platter to serve.

Masala Khitchri
Soft Rice and Yellow Mung Beans with Spices

Serves 8

Khitchri, in all its manifestations, is Indian comfort food. Its texture, soft and porridge-like, takes me back to my childhood. Essentially, it is a mixture of dal and rice cooked with plenty of water to make it the consistency of oatmeal (porridge to those of us who grew up with British terminology), then enhanced with a dollop of butter or, in this case, spiked with spices. I make this version for lunch at least once a week and eat it with plain yogurt and a little lemon pickle. A crunchy papadum adds the finishing touch.

❋

Tip

Khitchri will stiffen as it cools. Reheat in microwave before adding a little water to restore consistency.

1 ¼ cups	yellow mung beans (yellow mung dal)	300 mL
1 ¼ cups	long-grain rice	300 mL
2 tsp	salt	10 mL
2 tbsp	vegetable oil	25 mL
1 ½ tsp	cumin seeds	7 mL
¾ tsp	turmeric	4 mL
½ to ¾ tsp	cayenne pepper	2 to 4 mL

1. Clean and pick through beans for any small stones and grit. Rinse several times in cold water until water is fairly clear.

2. Drain beans and transfer to a large saucepan along with rice. Add 7 cups (1.75 L) water and salt. Bring to a boil over high heat. Reduce heat to medium and cook, partially covered, until mixture is very soft and water is almost absorbed, 25 to 30 minutes.

3. In a small saucepan, heat oil over medium heat. Sauté cumin seeds for 30 seconds. Stir in turmeric and cayenne pepper. Sauté for 10 seconds. Pour immediately into khitchri. Stir well to mix. Remove from heat and serve with plain yogurt or a raita (yogurt salad).

Upma
Semolina with Vegetables

One of the traditional south Indian breakfast offerings, this recipe is a Sunday brunch dish in my home. Accompanied with a crispy roasted papadum, a spicy pickle or chutney and cooling yogurt, it is a basic comfort food.

✼

♦ *Large wok or saucepan*

2 tbsp	vegetable oil	25 mL
2 tsp	mustard seeds	10 mL
2 tbsp	split yellow peas (channa dal)	25 mL
1	whole dried red chili	1
10 to 12	fresh curry leaves (optional)	10 to 12
2 tbsp	slivered peeled gingerroot	25 mL
1 tbsp	finely sliced green chilies, preferably serranos	15 mL
2 cups	chopped onions (2 to 3)	500 mL
1 cup	chopped red or green bell pepper	250 mL
¾ cup	frozen peas, thawed	175 mL
2½ tsp	salt or to taste	12 mL
2 cups	instant cream of wheat (sooji or rava)	500 mL
3 to 4 tbsp	lemon juice	45 to 60 mL
½ cup	cilantro, chopped, divided	125 mL
¼ cup	cashews	50 mL

1. In a wok or large saucepan, heat oil over high heat until almost smoking. Add mustard seeds and cover immediately. When seeds stop popping in a few seconds, uncover and reduce heat to medium. Immediately add split yellow peas, red chili and curry leaves, if using. Sauté for 30 seconds. Add ginger and sliced chilies. Sauté for 1 minute. Stir in onions and sauté until soft, about 5 minutes. Mix in bell pepper, peas and salt. Cook for 3 to 4 minutes.

2. Add cream of wheat and mix well. Add 3 cups (750 mL) hot water all at once, stirring vigorously until mixed. Reduce heat to low. Cover and cook for 2 to 3 minutes.

3. Remove from heat and stir in lemon juice and all but 2 tbsp (25 mL) of the cilantro. Scatter in cashews.

4. Spoon into a large bowl and sprinkle with remaining cilantro. Serve hot or at room temperature with yogurt and Indian pickles or chutney.

Fragrant Rice Layered with Curried Chicken

Hyderabadi Chicken Biriyani

• Preheat oven to 400°F (200°C)
• Large ovenproof casserole with tight-fitting lid

Serves 10 to 12

Arguably the most recognized of Moghul rice preparations, biriyanis are elaborate dishes combining chicken or lamb with exotic ingredients and spices, layered with basmati rice perfumed with saffron. They are a must for weddings and festive occasions. There are even special biriyani cooks who are hired to prepare this specialty for several hundred invitees. Traditionally, this dish is served without side dishes, accompanied only by a raita known as pachadi (see recipe, below).

❋

TIP

To make pachadi: Stir together 1½ cups (375 mL) chopped tomatoes, ¾ cup (175 mL) chopped onions, 3 tbsp (45 mL) cilantro, chopped and 2 cups (500 mL) plain yogurt. Season with salt and freshly ground black pepper.

2 cups	plain yogurt, at room temperature	500 mL
2 tbsp	minced green chilies, preferably serranos	25 mL
1½ tbsp	minced peeled gingerroot	22 mL
1½ tbsp	minced garlic	22 mL
6	large black cardamom pods, seeds only	6
16	whole cloves	16
3	cinnamon sticks, each 2 inches (5 cm) long	3
1 tsp	black peppercorns	5 mL
¼ tsp	turmeric	1 mL
6½ tsp	salt or to taste, divided	32 mL
12	skinless chicken thighs (3½ to 4 lbs/1.75 to 2 kg) or 1 chicken, skinned and cut into 12 pieces	12
1 cup	milk	250 mL
1 tsp	saffron threads	5 mL
3 cups	Indian basmati rice	750 mL
3 tbsp	vegetable oil	45 mL
8 cups	chopped onions (about 2 lbs/1 kg)	2 L
1½ tsp	garam masala	7 mL
3 cups	mint leaves, chopped, divided	750 mL
4 to 5	whole green chilies (optional)	4 to 5
¼ cup	vegetable oil	50 mL
2	hard-cooked eggs, quartered	2
2 tbsp	fried cashews (see Tip, right)	25 mL
2 tbsp	fried raisins (see Tip, right)	25 mL
1	tomato, quartered	1

1. Stir yogurt to a creamy consistency. Combine with chilies, ginger, garlic, cardamom, cloves, cinnamon, peppercorns, turmeric and 2½ tsp (12 mL) of the salt. Add chicken. Mix well. Cover and set aside for 1 hour in the refrigerator.

TIP

To fry raisins and cashews: Heat 1 tbsp (15 mL) vegetable oil in a skillet over medium heat. Stir in 2 tbsp (25 mL) nuts and 2 tbsp (25 mL) raisins. Sauté until nuts are golden and raisins plump up, about 2 minutes. Remove with slotted spoon and set aside.

2. Heat milk in a saucepan over medium heat until very hot. Stir in saffron threads and set aside.

3. Place rice in a bowl with plenty of cold water and swish vigorously with fingers. Drain. Repeat process 4 or 5 times until water is fairly clear. Cover with 3 to 4 inches (7.5 to 10 cm) water and soak for 10 to 15 minutes.

4. Fill a large saucepan three-quarters full with water. Add remaining salt. Bring to a boil over high heat. Drain rice and add to saucepan. Return to a boil and cook until rice is cooked on the outside but uncooked in the center, 2 to 3 minutes. Do not overcook. Drain immediately and spread in a shallow pan to cool.

5. Meanwhile, in another large saucepan, heat 3 tbsp (45 mL) oil over medium-high heat. Sauté onions until they begin to color. Reduce heat to medium and continue to sauté until very dark brown. This entire process can take up to 45 minutes.

6. Meanwhile, place chicken with marinade in a separate saucepan. Cover and bring to a boil over low heat. Remove from heat and leave covered.

7. *To assemble:* Spread half of the browned onions on bottom of ovenproof casserole with tight-fitting lid. Layer with chicken with marinade on top. Sprinkle with garam masala. Spread half of the rice over chicken. Layer remaining onion, half of the chopped mint and the whole green chilies, if using. Top with remaining rice and mint. Pour saffron milk evenly over entire surface. Drizzle ¼ cup (50 mL) oil on top. Cover casserole tightly with foil before putting on lid. Bake in preheated oven for 1 hour. Turn off oven and let rest for 10 minutes, without peeking.

8. *To serve:* Carefully spoon onto large platter. Arrange chicken pieces on top of rice and, if desired, discard whole cloves, cinnamon sticks and whole green chilies. Arrange egg quarters decoratively on top. Sprinkle with cashews and raisins. Garnish with tomato quarters.

Poha
Pressed Rice with Peas and Potatoes

Poha is a favorite of the people of Maharashtra, the largest state in western India. I make a light lunch of it, but it is perfect as a snack any time and is often packed for school lunches.

TIP

Poha is pressed rice made from parboiled rice, which is dried and pressed. It is available in Indian stores in packages of thick or thin flakes. Thin poha is preferrable for this recipe.

◆ *Large wok or saucepan*

2 tbsp	vegetable oil	25 mL
1 tsp	mustard seeds	5 mL
¼ tsp	asafetida (hing)	1 mL
3	whole cloves	3
6	black peppercorns	6
1	whole dried red chili, broken in half	1
1 tsp	cumin seeds	5 mL
10 to 12	fresh curry leaves (optional)	10 to 12
2 tsp	chopped green chilies, preferably serranos	10 mL
½ tsp	minced peeled gingerroot	2 mL
¾ cup	coarsely chopped onion	175 mL
¾ cup	diced peeled potatoes	175 mL
¾ tsp	turmeric	4 mL
1 tsp	salt or to taste	5 mL
¾ cup	frozen peas, thawed	175 mL
2 cups	thin dried flaked rice (poha) (see Tip, left)	500 mL
⅓ cup	cilantro, chopped	75 mL
2 tbsp	grated unsweetened coconut, fresh or frozen, thawed (optional)	25 mL
¼ cup	lime or lemon juice	50 mL
1 tsp	granulated sugar	5 mL
	Lemon wedges	

1. In a large wok or saucepan, heat oil over high heat until almost smoking. Add mustard seeds and cover immediately. When seeds stop popping in a few seconds, sprinkle in asafetida. Immediately reduce heat to medium. Add cloves, peppercorns, red chili, cumin seeds, curry leaves, if using, green chilies and ginger. Sauté for 1 minute. Add onion and sauté until translucent, about 5 minutes.

2. Add potatoes, turmeric and salt. Drizzle in 2 tbsp (25 mL) water. Reduce heat to low. Cover and cook until potatoes are almost soft, about 10 minutes.

3. Add peas and mix well. Cover and cook for 5 minutes. Place flaked rice in a colander and rinse briefly under cold water, gently running fingers through rice to allow water to run freely. Handle carefully as wet flaked rice is rather fragile. Shake out excess water and add immediately to pan. Add cilantro and coconut, if using. Remove from heat.

4. Stir together lime juice and sugar until sugar is dissolved. Add to flaked rice mixture, mixing gently and taking care not to break flakes. Serve with lemon wedges.

Sial Bread
Savory Indian Bread Pudding

This appetizing dish is ideal for brunch or as a unique side dish with poultry or fish. For a one-dish meal, add cooked shredded chicken to layers.

- ◆ *Preheat oven to 400°F (200°C)*
- ◆ *13-by 9-inch (3 L) baking pan, coated with vegetable spray*

1 tbsp	vegetable oil	15 mL
1 tsp	mustard seeds	5 mL
4 cups	finely sliced onions (4 to 5)	1 L
1 tsp	minced green chilies, preferably serranos	5 mL
6 cups	Roma tomato wedges, ¹⁄₂ inch (1 cm) thick	1.5 L
¹⁄₂ cup	cilantro, coarsely chopped, divided	125 mL
¹⁄₂ tsp	turmeric	2 mL
1 ¹⁄₂ tsp	salt or to taste	7 mL
12	thick slices bread, such as Italian (about 8 oz/250 g)	12
1 ¹⁄₂ cups	buttermilk	375 mL

1. In a large saucepan, heat oil over high heat until almost smoking. Add mustard seeds and cover immediately. When seeds stop popping in a few seconds, add onions and chilies. Mix well. Reduce heat to medium and cook, stirring, until onions are soft, 6 to 8 minutes. Do not brown.

2. Stir in tomatoes, ¹⁄₄ cup (50 mL) of the cilantro, turmeric and salt. Mix well. Cover and cook until tomatoes are soft, 6 to 8 minutes. Coarsely mash mixture. There should not be any liquid separating from mixture.

3. Spread a thin layer of tomato mixture on bottom of prepared pan. Dip bread in buttermilk to soak both sides. (Do not leave in buttermilk longer than 1 minute as bread will get too soft.) Arrange bread in a layer on top of mixture. Spread generous layer of tomato mixture over bread. Repeat with remaining bread slices dipped in buttermilk. Spread remaining tomato mixture on top. Sprinkle with remaining cilantro. Bake, uncovered, in preheated oven until golden, 25 to 30 minutes.

Atta
Basic Whole Wheat Dough

> **Makes enough dough for 16 chapatis, 10 parathas or 10 stuffed parathas**

This simplest of doughs, made from finely milled whole wheat, is the basis of a variety of everyday Indian breads. Chapati, also called roti (though that is also the generic word for all breads), is made daily in Indian homes, and parathas — both plain and stuffed — are very popular, too.

TIP

Chapati flour (atta) is whole wheat flour that has been very finely milled. Whole wheat flour from supermarkets or health food stores is coarse ground in comparison and lacks the natural sweetness; it is not suitable for chapatis. Chapati flour is available prepackaged in Indian grocery stores.

3 cups	chapati flour (atta) (see Tip, left)	750 mL
½ tsp	salt	2 mL
2 tbsp	vegetable oil	25 mL
¾ to 1 cup	lukewarm water (approx.)	175 to 250 mL

Food processor method

1. In a food processor with metal blade, combine flour and salt. Process for 5 seconds. Drizzle in oil. With machine running, pour in ¾ cup (175 mL) lukewarm water in a thin steady stream for 30 seconds. Scrape down sides of bowl. Gradually drizzle in more of the water in 3 or 4 additions, stopping every 20 seconds to check consistency of dough. Add just enough water until dough sticks together when pinched between thumb and forefinger. Process until dough forms a ball. Knead for 1 minute longer and turn off motor. The dough should be smooth and soft. Transfer dough to work surface and pat until perfectly smooth. Place in a bowl, cover with a damp cloth and let rest in a warm place for at least 30 minutes. (The dough can be made a day ahead and stored in the refrigerator in an airtight container. Let come to room temperature before using.)

Hand method

1. Sift flour and salt onto a large flat pizza pan. Drizzle oil on top and mix in with fingertips. Make a well in the center and add lukewarm water a little at a time while mixing the flour from the sides into the center. Use a circular motion with your fingers to incorporate all the flour. When you have added enough water to form a crumbly mixture, work it into a smooth dough. Add more water if necessary, a little at a time, kneading until dough is soft and smooth. Place in a bowl, cover with a damp cloth and let rest for 30 minutes. (The dough can be made a day ahead and stored in the refrigerator in an airtight container. Let come to room temperature before using.)

Chapati or Roti
Whole Wheat Griddle Bread

Chapati flour is very finely milled durum whole wheat. Chapati is the everyday bread of Indians, made daily in home kitchens.

TIPS

The correct temperature of the griddle is very important. If too hot, the chapati will burn before it cooks through. If too cold, it will take too long to brown and will become dry and tough.

◆

Chapatis can be made ahead, wrapped in foil and stored in the refrigerator for several days or frozen for several weeks. To reheat, place a stack of 4 in the microwave, covered, for 40 to 45 seconds. Or wrap in foil and warm in a 250°F (120°C) oven for 6 to 8 minutes.

1	batch Basic Whole Wheat Dough (Atta) (see recipe, page 47)	1
1/2 cup	chapati flour (atta)	125 mL
4 tsp	vegetable oil or melted butter	20 mL

1. On a clean surface, knead dough for 2 to 3 minutes. Roll into a 1½-inch (4 cm) thick rope. Pinch off 1-inch (2.5 cm) sections and roll into small balls. Place on a plate and cover with a damp cloth.

2. Heat a dry griddle or heavy skillet over medium-high heat for about 5 minutes.

3. Keep chapati flour in a small dish nearby. Sprinkle generous pinch on work surface and spread into a circle with your hand. Flatten ball of dough between your palms to ½-inch (1 cm) thick circle. Place on work surface and use rolling pin to roll into 7- to 8-inch (17.5 cm to 20 cm) circle (chapati). Lift a few times while rolling, sprinkling with just a hint of flour so chapati does not stick to surface.

4. Place chapati on hot dry griddle and cook for 1 minute. Flip and make sure some brown spots have appeared on cooked surface. If not, increase heat slightly. Cook second side for 30 to 40 seconds, pressing down on edges with crumpled paper towel. There should be a few brown spots on both sides. Transfer to a piece of foil or a dish towel and rub surface quickly with ¼ tsp (1 mL) oil. Repeat with remaining dough, keeping cooked chapatis covered and warm.

Paratha

Whole Wheat Griddle-Fried Bread

	batch Basic Whole Wheat Dough (Atta) (see recipe, page 47)	1
1/3 cup	vegetable oil, divided	75 mL
	Chapati flour for dusting	

Makes 10 parathas

Everyone loves a paratha, plain or stuffed. The dough is the same as for chapati, but parathas are flaky. They are ideal to pack for a picnic, a school lunch or, as Indians love to do, for a train journey.

TIP

Adjust heat to cook each paratha in 2 to 3 minutes. If it takes longer, parathas will become stiff. The layers of oil separate the dough and make this a soft bread on the inside and crisp and lightly browned on the outside. Parathas can be made several hours ahead, wrapped in foil and reheated in 250°F (120°C) oven. They can also be wrapped in foil when cool and refrigerated for 2 days or frozen for up to 3 months. Reheat refrigerated parathas in 250°F (120°C) oven for 10 minutes and frozen parathas for 20 minutes or until heated through.

1. Keep oil in a bowl near griddle, with a pastry brush at hand. Heat a dry griddle or heavy skillet over medium heat for 5 minutes.

2. Knead dough briefly. Divide into 10 portions and roll into balls. Keep covered.

3. Flatten one ball between palms into 1/2-inch (1 cm) thick circle. Dust generously with flour and shake off excess. Place on work surface and use rolling pin to roll into oval about 3 to 4 inches (7.5 to 10 cm) long. Brush generously with oil. With thumb and forefinger, pinch oval in center so fingers come together. Join oiled sides together by flipping one side over the other. You should now have a circle again. Brush again with oil and fold to make a half circle. Brush again with oil and fold to quarter circle. Roll out to 1/8-inch (0.25 cm) thickness. Paratha will not be circular.

4. Place paratha on griddle and cook for 2 minutes and flip. There should be brown spots. Cook second side for 2 minutes, making sure there are brown spots. Brush first side generously with oil and flip again. Cook, pressing down with a spatula so oil on underside will fry the paratha, for about 1 minute. Brush top with oil and flip and cook in the same manner. When paratha is cooked through, transfer to a dish and keep warm. Repeat with remaining dough and oil.

Aloo Paratha
Potato-Stuffed Griddle-Fried Bread

1	batch Basic Whole Wheat Dough (Atta) (see recipe, page 47)	1
STUFFING		
1 lb	all-purpose potatoes (about 3)	500 g
1/2 tsp	cumin powder	2 mL
1/2 tsp	turmeric	2 mL
1 tsp	salt or to taste	5 mL
1/2 cup	vegetable oil, divided	125 mL
2 tsp	chopped green chilies, preferably serranos	10 mL
3 tbsp	cilantro, chopped	45 mL
	Chapati flour, for dusting	

Makes 10 parathas

My grandchildren's faces light up when they hear their dinner is Aloo Paratha and yogurt. Parathas are a national favorite, and Aloo Parathas are without doubt number one.

TIP

Parathas can be refrigerated when cool, wrapped in foil, for 3 to 4 days or frozen for 2 to 3 months. Reheat refrigerated parathas in 250°F (120°C) oven for 10 minutes and frozen parathas for 20 minutes or until heated through.

1. *Stuffing:* Boil whole potatoes in their skins in a large saucepan of boiling water until soft, 20 to 25 minutes. When cool enough to handle, peel and mash. Set aside.

2. In a small bowl, mix together cumin, turmeric and salt. Set aside.

3. Heat 2 tbsp (25 mL) of the oil in a skillet over medium heat. Stir in chilies. Sauté for 1 minute. Add spice mix. Stir-fry for 20 seconds. Add potatoes. Remove from heat and mix in cilantro.

4. Set aside remaining oil in bowl with pastry brush nearby for assembly.

5. Heat a dry griddle or heavy skillet on medium-high heat for 5 minutes. Knead dough briefly. Divide into 10 portions. Roll each into a ball, cover with a cloth and set aside. Divide stuffing into 10 portions. Working with one ball at a time, flatten to shape the cup of your palm, to a circle about 4 inches (10 cm) in diameter. Place one portion of the stuffing in the center then pull dough gently together to cover filling and make a ball. Seal well and flatten between your palms into a disc, keeping seam on one side.

6. Dust disc with flour. With seam side down, roll gently to $\frac{1}{4}$-inch (0.5 cm) thick circle. Cook on griddle until brown spots form, 2 to 3 minutes. Flip and cook for 2 to 3 minutes longer, adjusting heat as necessary to prevent burning. Brush cooked side with oil and flip. Press gently with spatula to fry oiled side for 2 minutes. Brush other side, flip and fry in same manner. Transfer to a dish and keep warm. Repeat with remaining parathas.

Puri
Whole Wheat Puffed Bread

Makes
12 to 14 puris

Puri is a magical bread, puffed and filled with steam. Sensuous and light as a feather, it almost melts in your mouth when freshly made. Sadly, puris deflate rather quickly; though still good, the deflated ones cannot compare with just-made puris. A popular everyday bread, it is wonderful for scooping up morsels of food.

❋

TIP

Puris will deflate almost immediately but are still very good. The tapping action is most important or else they will not inflate with steam but remain flat.

- *Deep-fryer or wok*
- *Candy/deep-fry thermometer*

	Vegetable oil for deep-frying	
1	batch Basic Whole Wheat Dough (Atta) (see recipe, page 47)	1
1/2 cup	chapati flour (atta) (approx.)	125 mL

1. Heat oil to 350°F (180°C) in a deep-fryer or wok. Meanwhile, knead dough briefly. Divide dough in half. Keep one half covered. Sprinkle work surface lightly with flour and roll dough as thinly as possible. With a cookie cutter (or lid of jar about 3 to 4 inches/7.5 to 10 cm in diameter), cut out circles (puris). Slip into hot oil, one at a time. Tap top of puri rapidly with slotted spoon; within seconds it will begin to puff up. Turn over once and fry for another 10 seconds. Remove and drain on paper towels. Repeat with remaining dough. Serve hot.

Beans and Lentils

L ENTILS, OR DALS, as they are called in India, are a very important part of the
Indian diet. A primary source of protein for vegetarians, dals are consumed in
some form at almost every meal. The variety of dals is endless. They can be cooked
to a thick, paste-like consistency or a thin and soupy one. They can be cooked by
themselves or with vegetables or meat. Dals soaked overnight and puréed in the
blender make an amazing batter that can be turned into an endless variety of
savory pancakes, with an assortment of toppings or stuffings.

    A small variety of chickpeas (garbanzo beans), commercially ground into flour
called besan, is one of the most important ingredients for Indian cooking. It is as
close to a magical ingredient as you can get. Stirred into water, it makes an egg-free
dipping batter used for pakoras (fritters); made into a smooth paste, it is used to
thicken curries; and mixed with flour from grains, it makes wonderful flatbreads.

    I have chosen dishes that are not only delicious and easy but which also
illustrate the variety in textures, flavors and, of course, taste that beans and lentils
can provide.

❋   ❋   ❋

Yellow Mung Bean Soup
Mung Dal Soup

This is the quintessential comfort food of my childhood, the dish I crave even today when I return from a long trip. Packed with nutrients and flavors, it is the vegetarian equivalent of Mom's chicken soup.

TIPS

Soup can be refrigerated for up to 3 days. It will thicken when cooled or chilled. Do not add any additional water until reheated to serving temperature.

◆

If desired, cook a little thicker and serve over rice.

1 cup	yellow mung beans (yellow mung dal)	250 mL
½ tsp	turmeric	2 mL
1 cup	chopped tomato	250 mL
¼ cup	cilantro, chopped	50 mL
1 tsp	salt or to taste	5 mL
1½ tsp	vegetable oil	7 mL
1 tsp	cumin seeds	5 mL

1. Clean and pick through beans for any small stones and grit. Rinse several times in cold water until water is fairly clear.

2. Drain beans and transfer to a large saucepan. Add 6 cups (1.5 L) water and soak for 15 minutes. Bring to a boil over medium heat, skimming froth off surface. Stir in turmeric and adjust heat to maintain a gentle boil. Cook, partially covered, until dal is very soft, 15 to 20 minutes. Purée using an immersion blender or whisk vigorously to a batter-like consistency. Add tomato, cilantro and salt.

3. In a small saucepan, heat oil over medium heat. Add cumin seeds and sauté until seeds turn a little darker, about 30 seconds. Add to dal and simmer, uncovered, for 5 minutes. Dal should be thick but runny. Add hot water if necessary for desired consistency.

Makhni Dal
Buttery Mung Dal

Serves 6 to 8

This dish from my ethnic Sindhi cuisine is still the most requested dal when my sons visit. The name is derived from its "buttery" appearance and creamy texture. There is no butter in the recipe and minimal fat, yet it tastes rich! The secret is in the way it is cooked.

❋

TIP

The starch in this particular dal makes it creamy when pressed through a sieve, which you could do if you don't have an immersion blender.

1 ½ cups	yellow mung beans (yellow mung dal)	375 mL
¼ tsp	turmeric	1 mL
1 ½ tsp	salt or to taste	7 mL
1 ½ tsp	coriander powder	7 mL
¾ tsp	cumin powder	4 mL
½ tsp	cayenne pepper	2 mL
½ tsp	garam masala	2 mL
1 ½ tbsp	vegetable oil	22 mL
3 tbsp	coarsely chopped garlic	45 mL
1 ½ tsp	mango powder (amchur) (optional)	7 mL
¾ tsp	freshly ground black pepper	4 mL

1. Clean and pick through beans for any small stones and grit. Rinse several times in cold water until water is fairly clear. Soak in 4 cups (1 L) water in a large saucepan for 10 minutes.

2. Bring to a boil over medium heat, skimming froth off surface. Stir in turmeric and adjust heat to maintain a gentle boil. Cook, partially covered, until dal is very soft, about 20 minutes. Stir in salt.

3. Remove from heat. Using an immersion blender, blend until creamy and smooth. Alternately, transfer to blender or press through a sieve (see Tip, left). Texture should be very thick, like lightly whipped cream.

4. Return mixture to very low heat. Pile coriander, cumin, cayenne pepper and garam masala in the center of the dal. Do not stir to mix.

5. In a small saucepan, heat oil over medium heat. Sauté garlic until golden, 3 to 4 minutes. Pour over spices. Remove from heat.

6. Gently transfer dal to a serving bowl, trying not to disturb the spice and garlic mixture. Sprinkle mango powder, if using, and pepper over entire surface of dish. Serve with Indian bread.

Toor Dal Soup with Vegetables

Yellow Lentil Soup with Vegetables

Here's a soul-satisfying soup packed with vitamins and the goodness of vegetables. Plus the dal makes it high in protein and fiber as well.

1 cup	yellow lentils (toor dal)	250 mL
1 tsp	turmeric	5 mL
1 cup	chopped tomato	250 mL
1 cup	cubed potato	250 mL
1 cup	sliced carrot, 1/4-inch (0.5 cm) thick slices	250 mL
8	green beans, cut into 1-inch (2.5 cm) pieces	8
1/4 tsp	cayenne pepper	1 mL
1 tsp	salt or to taste	5 mL
2 tbsp	vegetable oil	25 mL
1 tsp	cumin seeds	5 mL
1 tbsp	chopped garlic	15 mL
1/2 cup	chopped onion	125 mL
1 1/2 cups	steamed rice	375 mL
1/3 cup	cilantro, chopped	75 mL
	Lemon wedges	

1. Clean and pick through lentils for any small stones and grit. Rinse several times in cold water until water is fairly clear.

2. Drain and transfer lentils to a large saucepan. Add 3 cups (750 mL) water and soak for 10 minutes. Bring to a boil, uncovered, over medium heat, skimming froth off surface. Cook, partially covered, until dal is soft and mushy, about 30 minutes. Purée in blender or using immersion blender, or whisk vigorously to batter-like consistency.

3. Return to pan. Stir in another 3 cups (750 mL) water and turmeric. Add tomato, potato, carrot, green beans, cayenne pepper and salt. Cover and return to a boil over medium–high heat. Reduce heat to medium–low and simmer for 12 to 15 minutes.

4. Meanwhile, in a small saucepan, heat oil over medium–high heat. Add cumin seeds. Sauté until cumin is fragrant and a shade darker, about 30 seconds. Add garlic and sauté for 1 minute. Add onion and cook until golden, about 10 minutes.

5. Pour mixture into dal and simmer, covered, until vegetables are tender, about 5 minutes.

6. Place 2 to 3 tbsp (25 to 45 mL) rice in each bowl. Top with dal and vegetable mixture. Garnish with cilantro. Serve with lemon wedges on the side.

Uma's Toor Dal
Uma's Puréed Yellow Lentils

Serves 4 to 6

A young friend of my daughter-in-law's gave me this recipe. It is an excellent everyday dal with a hint of tanginess.

TIP

Dal will stiffen when refrigerated and loosen again when reheated. Stir in additional water if needed, only after reheating.

1 cup	yellow lentils (toor dal)	250 mL
2 tsp	salt or to taste, divided	10 mL
1 1/2 tbsp	vegetable oil	22 mL
1 1/2 tsp	mustard seeds	7 mL
1	cinnamon stick, 2 inches (5 cm) long	1
4	whole cloves	4
1/4 tsp	asafetida (hing)	1 mL
4 cups	chopped tomatoes (about 4)	1 L
2	green chilies, preferably serranos, cut in half lengthwise, but left attached at the stem end	2
2 tsp	minced peeled gingerroot	10 mL
1 tsp	coriander powder	5 mL
1/2 tsp	cumin powder	2 mL
1/2 tsp	cayenne pepper	2 mL
1/3 cup	cilantro, chopped	75 mL
8 to 10	fresh curry leaves (optional)	8 to 10
1 tbsp	jaggery (gur) or brown sugar	15 mL
3 to 4 tbsp	lime or lemon juice	45 to 60 mL

1. Clean and pick through lentils for any small stones and grit. Rinse several times in cold water until water is fairly clear. Soak in 4 cups (1 L) water in a large saucepan for 10 minutes.

2. Bring to a boil over medium-high heat, skimming froth off surface. Reduce heat to maintain a gentle boil. Cook, partially covered, until soft and mushy, about 20 minutes. Stir in 1 tsp (5 mL) salt. Using an immersion blender or in a blender, blend until smooth.

3. In another large saucepan, heat oil over high heat until a couple of mustard seeds thrown in start to sputter. Add remaining mustard seeds and cover immediately.

4. When seeds stop popping in a few seconds, uncover and add cinnamon, cloves and asafetida. Sauté for 30 seconds. Reduce heat to medium and add tomatoes, chilies, ginger, remaining salt, coriander, cumin and cayenne pepper. Cook until tomatoes are soft, 7 to 8 minutes.

5. Pour dal into tomato mixture. Stir in cilantro, curry leaves, if using, jaggery and lime juice. Cover and simmer to allow flavors to blend, about 15 minutes. Adjust seasonings before serving. Remove cinnamon stick and cloves, if desired. Serve hot with rice.

Channna Dal with Tamarind Chutney

Split Yellow Peas with Tamarind Chutney

Serves 8		

This recipe is from my ethnic cuisine: Sindhi cooking. Channa dal is cooked until it is soft but, unlike other dals, it is seldom puréed. Its soft but firm texture lends itself to interesting combinations. The blandness of the dal is the perfect foil for the zippy tamarind chutney.

❋

TIP

This is not a soupy dal. When dal is soft, all water should be absorbed and dal should not get mushy. The amount of water is critical in this recipe, but not so in soupy dal dishes.

2 cups	split yellow peas (channa dal)	500 mL
1 tsp	turmeric	5 mL
2 tsp	salt or to taste	10 mL
1 tbsp	mango powder (amchur) or ¼ cup (50 mL) freshly squeezed lemon juice	15 mL
1 tbsp	coriander powder	15 mL
2 tsp	cumin powder	10 mL
1 tsp	garam masala	5 mL
1 tsp	cayenne pepper	5 mL
2½ tbsp	vegetable oil	32 mL
½ cup	Tamarind Chutney (see recipe, page 168)	125 mL
1	medium onion, cut into thin rounds and separated into rings	1
2 tbsp	cilantro, chopped	25 mL

1. Clean and pick through peas for any small stones and grit. Rinse several times in cold water until water is fairly clear. Soak in 3 cups (750 mL) water in a large saucepan for 20 minutes (see Tip, left).

2. Bring to a boil over medium–high heat, skimming froth off surface. Reduce heat to medium. Stir in turmeric and simmer, partially covered, until dal is tender and water is absorbed, about 30 minutes. Avoid stirring too much as dal should not be mushy. When almost cooked and little water remains, stir in salt. Dal should be dry. Remove from heat.

3. In a small bowl, mix together mango powder, coriander, cumin, garam masala and cayenne pepper. Sprinkle on top of dal and cover.

4. In a small saucepan, heat oil over medium–high heat until very hot. Pour over spices and let stand, covered, for 5 minutes.

5. Transfer dal to a serving dish, trying to keep the spices on top. Drizzle tamarind chutney over dal. Top with onion rings. Sprinkle with cilantro. Serve with an Indian bread.

Rajma
North Indian-Style Kidney Beans

Serves 6 to 8		

Kidney beans are a favorite of the people of Punjab, where Rajma is eaten almost daily. Pressure cookers are used extensively to save on time and fuel. If you have one, this recipe will put it to good use.

TIP

Though it's unconventional, try adding bite-size pieces of boneless chicken in Step 4. It will turn Rajma into a one-dish meal.

2 cups	red kidney beans, rinsed and soaked overnight	500 mL
1 1/2 tbsp	vegetable oil	22 mL
1/2 tsp	asafetida (hing)	2 mL
3 cups	chopped tomatoes	750 mL
1/4 cup	plain nonfat yogurt	50 mL
2 tsp	coriander powder	10 mL
1 tsp	cumin powder	5 mL
1/2 tsp	turmeric	2 mL
2 tsp	salt or to taste	10 mL
1 tsp	garam masala	5 mL
1/2 cup	cilantro, chopped, divided	125 mL

1. Drain beans and place in a large saucepan. Add fresh water to cover by 3 inches (7.5 cm). Bring to boil over medium-high heat. Reduce heat to medium-low and simmer, partially covered, until beans are very tender, about 1 hour.

2. Meanwhile, in another saucepan, heat oil over medium-high heat. Add asafetida. When it stops sizzling in about 30 seconds, add tomatoes. Cook until tomatoes are very soft, 5 to 6 minutes. Mash with back of spoon.

3. Stir yogurt to a creamy consistency and add to tomatoes. Cook for 1 minute.

4. Stir in coriander, cumin, turmeric and salt. Reduce heat to medium-low and cook, stirring continuously to prevent burning, 4 to 5 minutes.

5. Drain beans, reserving liquid. Add beans to tomato mixture (masala) and mix well. Cook for 3 to 4 minutes. Pour in reserved liquid and simmer until gravy is desired thickness.

6. Remove from heat and sprinkle with garam masala and 1/4 cup (50 mL) of the cilantro. Garnish with remaining cilantro when serving. Serve with rice or bread.

Zucchini with Yellow Mung Beans

This is a delicious combination of a popular vegetable and one of my favorite dals. The recipe comes from a friend who visits every year and is an inveterate collector of family recipes.

❋

1 cup	yellow mung beans (yellow mung dal)	250 mL
2 tbsp	vegetable oil	25 mL
1 tsp	mustard seeds	5 mL
1 tsp	cumin seeds	5 mL
1/2 tsp	fenugreek seeds (methi)	2 mL
1/2 cup	sliced green onions (2 to 3)	125 mL
2 tsp	minced garlic	10 mL
2 tsp	minced peeled gingerroot	10 mL
2 cups	chopped tomatoes	500 mL
4 tsp	sambar powder	20 mL
1 tsp	coriander powder	5 mL
1/2 tsp	turmeric	2 mL
3	zucchini (about 1 1/2 lbs/750 g), sliced 1/4 inch (0.5 cm) thick	3
1 tsp	salt or to taste	5 mL
	Juice of 1 lime or 1/2 lemon	
1/2 cup	cilantro, chopped, divided	125 mL
1 tsp	garam masala	5 mL

1. Clean and pick through beans for any small stones and grit. Rinse several times in cold water until water is fairly clear. Soak in 4 cups (1 L) water in a large saucepan for 10 minutes.

2. Meanwhile, heat oil in a large saucepan over high heat until a couple of mustard seeds thrown in start to sputter. Add remaining mustard seeds and cover immediately. When seeds stop popping after a few seconds, reduce heat to medium. Add cumin and fenugreek seeds. Sauté for 20 to 30 seconds. Do not allow seeds to burn.

3. Stir in green onions, garlic and ginger. Sauté for 1 minute. Add tomatoes, sambar powder, coriander and turmeric. Mix well and sauté until tomatoes are soft, about 5 minutes.

4. Drain dal and add to onion mixture. Sauté for 3 to 4 minutes. Pour in 2 cups (500 mL) water. Cover and bring to a boil. Reduce heat to low and simmer, stirring occasionally, for 15 minutes.

5. Stir in zucchini and salt. Cover and cook, stirring occasionally, until vegetables and dal are soft, 15 to 20 minutes. Dal should be completely mushy and thickened.

6. Remove from heat. Stir in lime juice and all but 2 tbsp (25 mL) of the cilantro. Sprinkle with garam masala and cover for 5 minutes before serving. Garnish with remaining cilantro and serve with an Indian bread or rice.

Kali Dal or Dal Makhni
Buttery Black Beans

The Moghuls, who ruled India for more than three centuries and were renowned for their elegant architecture and cuisine, introduced rich ingredients such as nuts, cream and butter to Indian cuisine. Their influence is evident in this classic dish offered at all north Indian restaurants.

❋

1 cup	Indian black beans (sabat urad)	250 mL
1/3 cup	red kidney beans	75 mL
1 tbsp	minced green chilies, preferably serranos	15 mL
1 1/2 tbsp	minced peeled gingerroot	22 mL
3/4 cup	plain nonfat yogurt, at room temperature	175 mL
3/4 tsp	cornstarch	4 mL
1 1/2 tsp	salt or to taste	7 mL
1/4 cup	butter, softened	50 mL

1. Clean and pick through black and red beans for any small stones and grit. Rinse several times in cold water until water is fairly clear. Place in a large saucepan and add fresh water to cover by 3 inches (7.5 cm). Soak overnight.

2. Add 2 cups (500 mL) water to beans and soaking liquid. Add chilies and ginger. Partially cover and bring to a boil over medium–high high. (Do not cover completely as beans will boil over.) Reduce heat to maintain a gentle boil and cook until soft, about 1 hour.

3. Stir yogurt to a creamy consistency and combine with cornstarch. Set aside.

4. When beans are soft, stir in yogurt mixture and salt. Simmer to allow flavors to blend, about 10 minutes. Transfer warm dal to serving dish. Top with butter and allow to pool in middle as it melts. Serve with rice or an Indian bread.

Sindhi Chicken Curry (page 84)

Overleaf: Tandoori Chicken Salad (page 72) with Cucumber Raita *(Kakri Raita)* (page 162) and Chapatis (page 48)

Sindhi-Style Chickpeas

Sindhis love this dish and serve it at lunch and brunch. They even take it on picnics, where instead of spooning beans on top, bread is served individually and used to dunk in the beans. Tamarind chutney (see recipe, page 168) is often drizzled on top, for a variation.

❋

TIP

There should be enough gravy to soak into bread, which should be almost soggy.

2 cups	chickpeas (garbanzo beans), soaked overnight	500 mL
2 tbsp	vegetable oil	25 mL
6 cups	chopped onions (6 to 8)	1.5 L
1 cup	diced tomatoes	250 mL
1 1/2 tbsp	minced green chilies, preferably serranos	22 mL
2 tsp	minced peeled gingerroot	10 mL
4 tsp	cumin powder	20 mL
2 tsp	coriander powder	10 mL
2 tsp	cayenne pepper	10 mL
1/2 tsp	turmeric	2 mL
2 tsp	salt	10 mL
1/2 cup	Thai tamarind paste	125 mL
12	small soft dinner rolls, split in half	12
	Thinly sliced red onion rings	

1. Drain chickpeas and place in a large saucepan with 6 cups (1.5 L) water. Bring to a boil over medium–high heat. Reduce heat to maintain a gentle boil and cook, partially covered, until beans are soft, 45 minutes to 1 hour. Strain, reserving liquid.

2. In a large saucepan, heat oil over medium–high heat. Add onions and sauté until beginning to color, 8 to 10 minutes. Reduce heat to medium and sauté until deep golden, about 15 minutes.

3. Add tomatoes, chilies, ginger, cumin, coriander, cayenne, turmeric and salt. Cook for 3 to 4 minutes to soften tomatoes. Pour in 2 cups (500 mL) of the reserved liquid. Cover and bring to a boil. Reduce heat to medium-low. Simmer for 5 minutes. Mash mixture (masala) with back of spoon.

4. Mix in beans and tamarind. Add 1/2 cup (125 mL) liquid from beans. Cover and cook for 15 minutes. Mash a few beans against side of pan to thicken gravy.

5. Arrange rolls on platter. Spoon beans with gravy on top. Garnish with onion rings scattered over top.

Dry-Fried Lamb with Coconut Slices (page 98)

Sambar
South Indian Lentil and Vegetable Stew

Sambar is the signature lentil dish of the southern state of Tamilnadu. There are innumerable variations, but I prefer this hearty stew-like consistency to the more traditional, thinner, broth-like version with fewer vegetables. Also, I have added masoor dal (red lentils) to make it lighter to digest (see Tips, right). My family enjoys this hearty vegetable stew for Sunday lunch.

❋

1 cup	yellow lentils (toor dal)	250 mL
¹⁄₂ cup	red lentils (masoor dal)	125 mL
2 tbsp	vegetable oil	25 mL
2 tsp	mustard seeds	10 mL
¹⁄₄ tsp	asafetida (hing)	1 mL
1¹⁄₂ tbsp	minced peeled gingerroot	22 mL
1¹⁄₂ tbsp	sliced green chilies, preferably serranos	22 mL
1 tbsp	minced garlic	15 mL
5 to 6	green onions, finely sliced with some green	5 to 6
2 cups	eggplant chunks, about 1¹⁄₂ inches (4 cm)	500 mL
2	carrots, peeled and cut into 1-inch (2.5 cm) chunks	2
2	medium tomatoes, cut into 1-inch (2.5 cm) wedges	2
¹⁄₃ cup	cilantro, chopped	75 mL
1 tbsp	sambar powder	15 mL
³⁄₄ tsp	turmeric	4 mL
2 tsp	salt or to taste	10 mL
2 to 3 tbsp	Thai tamarind paste	25 to 45 mL

1. Clean and pick through lentils for any small stones and grit. Combine lentils and rinse several times in cold water until water is fairly clear. Soak in 4 cups (1 L) water in a large saucepan for 10 minutes.

2. Bring to a boil over medium–high heat, skimming froth off surface. Reduce heat to low and simmer, partially covered, until soft and mushy, about 30 minutes. Using an immersion blender or blender, blend until smooth.

Sambar freezes well for up to 3 months. Like all dals, it solidifies when chilled and should be reheated on low heat on the stove or in the microwave. It will loosen as it warms. Dilute with a little water if too thick after it is heated through.

◆

All dals are not created equal. Their "digestibility" varies greatly, depending on the amount of starch, protein and other nutrients. Yellow mung dal is the easiest to digest and is fed to babies at six months, whereas urad dal is the most difficult to digest.

3. Meanwhile, in a large saucepan, heat oil over high heat until a couple of mustard seeds thrown in start to sputter. Add remaining mustard seeds and cover immediately. Uncover after a few seconds when seeds stop popping.

4. Reduce heat to medium and add asafetida. Sauté for 30 seconds. Add ginger, chilies and garlic. Sauté for 1 minute. Add green onions and sauté for 2 minutes.

5. Stir in eggplant, carrots and tomatoes. Sauté until vegetables are coated and slightly seared, 3 to 4 minutes. Sprinkle with cilantro and sambar powder. Mix well and cook for 2 to 3 minutes.

6. Pour dal into vegetables. Stir in turmeric and salt. Cover and simmer until vegetables are cooked and flavors are blended, about 10 minutes. Stir in tamarind paste. Sambar should be consistency of creamy soup. If too thick, add water to dilute and heat through. Serve hot with rice.

Tomatochen Sar
Tomato Dal

As the name implies, this tasty dal is enhanced with lots of tomatoes. Simply seasoned, it is a favorite in Maharashtra, a large state in western India.

❋

1 cup	red lentils (masoor dal)	250 mL
2½ cups	chopped tomatoes (about 3)	625 mL
¼ tsp	turmeric	1 mL
1½ tsp	salt or to taste	7 mL
½ cup	cilantro, chopped	125 mL
1 tsp	minced peeled gingerroot	5 mL
1 tsp	minced garlic	5 mL
1 tbsp	vegetable oil	15 mL
½ tsp	mustard seeds	2 mL
½ tsp	cumin seeds	2 mL
2	dried red chilies, broken in half	2
8 to 10	fresh curry leaves (optional)	8 to 10

1. Clean and pick through lentils for any small stones and grit. Rinse several times in cold water until water is fairly clear. Soak in 4 cups (1 L) water in a large saucepan for 10 minutes.

2. Bring to a boil over medium-high heat, skimming froth off surface. Stir in tomatoes and turmeric. Reduce heat to medium-low and cook for 20 minutes. Sprinkle in salt and cook until dal is soft, about 10 minutes. With an immersion blender or in a blender, blend and return to a gentle boil. Stir in cilantro, ginger and garlic.

3. Meanwhile, in a small saucepan, heat oil over high heat until a couple of mustard seeds thrown in start to sputter. Add remaining mustard seeds and cover immediately. When seeds stop popping after a few seconds, uncover and reduce heat to medium. Add cumin seeds, chilies and curry leaves, if using. Sauté for 30 seconds. Pour immediately into dal. Cover and simmer for 10 minutes. Serve with rice.

Poultry and Meat

T HE MUTTONWALLA, OUR meat vendor, arrived at the front door every other morning like clockwork. When he arrived at 8:30, the cook would examine the meat, making sure it was fresh and lean, and place an order for the next delivery. The man selling eggs, the undawalla, appeared twice a week at our doorstep, while the fresh vegetable vendor, the sabziwalla, came almost daily. This system of home delivery was a way of life when I lived in India, and supplemented visits to the bazaar for staples. Fish and seafood, on the other hand always meant a trip to the fish market very early to get the fresh catch of the day.

Contrary to what is commonly believed, most Indians are not vegetarian. Religion plays a major role in dietary preferences, and even within the same geographical area there can be a wide variety of foods that are acceptable or taboo. In the almost 90 per cent vegetarian state of Gujerat, whose people are either Hindu or Jain (an offshoot of Hinduism), there are pockets of Muslims who have lived there for centuries and whose diet is mainly non-vegetarian. Kerala has three distinct cuisines, reflecting the three ethnic groups who live there: Hindus, Muslims (who are descendants of Arab traders who married locally and settled in the area hundreds of years ago) and a large community of Syrian Christians. All three have distinct cuisines, using, as always, local ingredients. In some parts of the country, Hindus are vegetarian. In others, such as in Kashmir, the Kashmiri Brahmins' (priests) diet includes several meat preparations. Even among Buddhists, there are those who eat meat and those who do not, just as there are North American vegetarians who eat fish and eggs and others who do not. However, there are very few vegans in India. Milk and milk products are considered sacred, as they are derived from the cow, considered sacred by Hindus. Milk and ghee (clarified butter) are used extensively in Hindu rituals, and sweets made with milk are a must at celebrations and religious ceremonies.

Goat meat, referred to as mutton, is the most commonly cooked red meat. In the north, lamb too is very popular. Beef is taboo for Hindus, and pork is shunned by Muslims and Hindus. Chicken, however, is widely available and enjoyed. Its versatility and universal acceptance have resulted in wonderful recipes from around the country, and I have picked some of my favorites.

In chicken recipes that call for slow simmering, I specify dark meat, preferably on the bone because it results in meltingly soft morsels full of mouth-watering flavors. White meat tends to get dry and stringy when braised and is better suited to stir-fried dishes. Chicken skin is never eaten. Always rinse chicken before cooking; I like to pat it dry. When you want to marinate chicken, try to plan ahead to allow chicken to air-dry in the refrigerator on a baking sheet lined with paper towels for an hour or longer. This will ensure that no moisture remains to dilute the marinade. I sometimes refrigerate it overnight.

Tandoori Chicken

Serves 8

A tandoor is a North Indian clay oven that is about three feet high, usually buried in the ground up to the neck. Live coals are placed in the bottom, and skewers with meat and poultry are angled at a suitable distance from the heat to cook them. It's the Indian version of a barbecue.

❊

TIPS

Tandoori chicken is best cooked on a charcoal grill. Buy split chickens or leg quarters if using this method. Grease barbecue grill and preheat to medium–high. Place chicken on grill and cook, covered, for 20 minutes. Turn and cook until juices run clear when chicken is pierced, 20 to 25 minutes.

◆

Ginger and garlic can be minced in a blender, grated on a ginger grater or purchased already prepared in jars.

◈ *Preheat oven to 375°F (190°C)*
◈ *Shallow baking pan, lined with foil*

16	skinless bone-in chicken thighs, or thighs and drumsticks (about 5 lbs/2.5 kg)	16
1 cup	plain nonfat yogurt	250 mL
	Juice of 2 lemons	
1 tbsp	minced peeled gingerroot	15 mL
1 tbsp	minced garlic	15 mL
2 tsp	coriander powder	10 mL
2 tsp	cumin powder	10 mL
2 tsp	garam masala	10 mL
1 tsp	cayenne pepper	5 mL
1 1/2 tsp	salt or to taste	7 mL
	Few drops red food coloring (optional)	
	Juice of 2 limes or additional lemons	
1	onion, cut into rings, for garnish	1
	Lemon wedges, for garnish	

1. Rinse chicken and pat dry. Cut long diagonal slits against the grain, almost to the bone.

2. In a shallow bowl, mix together yogurt, lemon juice, ginger, garlic, coriander, cumin, garam masala, cayenne pepper and salt. Add red food coloring, if using. Add chicken, turning to coat and making sure marinade goes into all slits. Cover and marinate in refrigerator for about 2 hours or for up to 12 hours.

3. Remove chicken from marinade and place in prepared shallow baking pan. Discard any remaining marinade. Bake in preheated oven until juices run clear when chicken is pierced, about 45 minutes.

4. Transfer pieces onto heated platter and squeeze lime juice on top while still warm. Discard accumulated juices. Garnish with sliced onion rings and lemon wedges.

Tandoori Chicken Salad

This is a delightful salad for summer meals or anytime you have leftover tandoori chicken. In fact, I recommend you make a double recipe of the chicken and use it for the salad the next day. It makes a delicious filling for a pita sandwich, topped with shredded lettuce and a dollop of yogurt. It is also a great picnic dish.

6 cups	shredded Tandoori Chicken (see recipe, page 71)	1.5 L
1 cup	julienne jicama or water chestnuts	250 mL
1/2 cup	finely sliced green onions, with some green	125 mL
1/3 cup	cilantro, chopped	75 mL
3 tbsp	toasted sesame seeds (see Tips, page 145)	45 mL
	Juice of 2 limes or lemons	
2 tsp	minced green chilies, preferably serranos (optional)	10 mL
	Boston lettuce	

1. Toss together chicken, jicama, green onions, cilantro, sesame seeds, lime juice and chilies, if using. Chill for at least 1 hour or for up to 3 hours.

2. Serve over lettuce or in lettuce "cups."

Chicken Tikka Masala

This dish was called Chicken Makhanwalla (Butter Chicken) until the British adopted it as their favorite Indian dish and its name morphed into this one. Chicken Tikka means "bite-size boneless chicken."

❋

TIPS

This dish is better prepared ahead. Let cool, cover and refrigerate for up to 4 days or freeze for up to 3 months. Reheat on very low heat or in microwave. (If made ahead, add fresh cilantro and a little additional garam masala and cumin before serving.)

◆

To toast cumin seeds: Spread seeds in a layer in a heavy dry skillet. Cook over medium heat, shaking skillet occasionally to toast evenly, until seeds are a little darker and aromatic, 3 to 4 minutes. Let cool. Grind to a powder in a spice grinder.

12	cooked tandoori chicken thighs (see recipe, page 71), divided	12
3	green chilies, preferably serranos	3
1	piece (1 inch/2.5 cm) peeled gingerroot	1
1	can (28 oz/796 mL) whole or diced tomatoes, including juice	1
½ cup	butter, divided	125 mL
2 tbsp	freshly ground toasted cumin seeds, divided (see Tips, left)	25 mL
2 tsp	paprika	10 mL
1 cup	whipping (35%) cream	250 mL
1½ tsp	salt or to taste	7 mL
2 tsp	garam masala	10 mL
¾ cup	cilantro, chopped	175 mL

1. Carefully debone cooked chicken, taking care not to shred it.

2. In a food processor, process chilies and ginger. Add tomatoes with juice and purée until smooth.

3. In a large saucepan, melt ¼ cup (50 mL) of the butter over medium heat. Add one-third of the chicken and sauté until edges begin to brown, 3 to 4 minutes. Transfer with a slotted spoon to a bowl. Brown remaining 2 batches of chicken in the same manner, adding 2 tbsp (25 mL) of the remaining butter as needed to prevent sticking.

4. Melt remaining 2 tbsp (25 mL) of butter in saucepan. Reduce heat to medium–low. Cook, stirring and scraping up all browned bits. Stir in 4 tsp (20 mL) of the cumin seeds and paprika. Stir rapidly for 1 minute.

5. Pour in tomato mixture and return to a gentle boil. Cook, uncovered, stirring frequently to allow flavors to blend, about 10 minutes. Add cream, salt, chicken and accumulated juices. Simmer, uncovered, stirring gently a few times and scraping bottom to prevent burning, until chicken is heated through, 10 to 12 minutes.

6. Stir in garam masala and remaining cumin. Remove from heat and cover. Let stand for 10 minutes before serving. Serve garnished with cilantro.

Coriander Chicken

Coriander is one of the most popular seasonings in the Indian lexicon of spices and herbs. Its sweet, nutty flavor complements meats and vegetables alike. This simple but so delicious recipe showcases the highly aromatic spice.

❋

TIPS

The key to success with this recipe lies in the freshly toasted and ground coriander seeds. The few extra minutes it takes to do this is well worth it. Do not use store-bought ground coriander.

To toast coriander seeds: Spread in a dry heavy skillet. Cook over medium heat, shaking skillet occasionally to toast evenly, until seeds are a little darker and aromatic, 4 to 5 minutes. Let cool. Grind to a powder in a spice grinder.

◆

If doubling recipe, cook in 2 batches.

12	skinless boneless chicken thighs, about 3 lbs (1.5 kg)	12
2 tbsp	minced peeled gingerroot	25 mL
2 tbsp	minced garlic	25 mL
2 tsp	salt or to taste	10 mL
	Juice of 1 lime or lemon	
3 tbsp	vegetable oil	45 mL
5 tbsp	coriander seeds, freshly toasted and powdered in spice grinder (to yield about ¼ cup/50 mL powder) (see Tips, left)	60 mL
1 tbsp	freshly ground black pepper	15 mL
2	green onions, finely sliced, with some green, for garnish	2

1. Rinse chicken and pat dry.

2. In a large bowl, combine ginger, garlic, salt and lime juice. Add chicken and toss to coat. Cover and marinate in refrigerator for 1 hour.

3. In a large saucepan, heat oil over medium–high heat. Add chicken with marinade and sauté until juices exuded from chicken cook down. When there is no more liquid, continue to brown chicken. The entire process will take 10 to 12 minutes.

4. Reduce heat to medium. Mix in coriander and pepper. Sauté for 2 minutes longer. If necessary, add water, 1 to 2 tbsp (15 to 25 mL) at a time, to prevent chicken from sticking to pan while browning.

5. Add ⅓ cup (75 mL) water. Cover and simmer until chicken is no longer pink inside, 8 to 10 minutes. Shake pan periodically to prevent burning. There should be no liquid left in the pan and a thick gravy should coat the chicken.

6. Garnish with green onions.

Pepper Chicken

Serves 8

Recipes in India are often closely guarded family secrets. Sometimes, though, a favorite recipe will accompany a bride to her new home. Many years ago, the wife of a young cousin introduced me to this dish from her family. The first time I tasted it, I thought it was incredible and, 30 years later, I still think so.

TIPS

Pepper Chicken is equally good as a curry. Do not reduce as much, leaving some of the yogurt gravy to spoon over rice. If planning to freeze, definitely leave extra gravy to spoon over chicken, to ensure it stays moist.

◆

To crack black peppercorns: Pound in a mortar and pestle or place in a heavy-duty resealable plastic bag and crack with a meat mallet or bottom of a saucepan until cracked. Do not grind.

12	skinless bone-in chicken thighs, or drumsticks and thighs (about 4 lbs/2 kg)	12
2 cups	plain nonfat yogurt	500 mL
2 tsp	cornstarch	10 mL
1 tbsp	minced peeled gingerroot	15 mL
1 tbsp	minced garlic	15 mL
2	minced green chilies, preferably serranos	2
2 tsp	salt or to taste	10 mL
1 cup	cilantro, chopped	250 mL
2 tbsp	vegetable oil	25 mL
1 tbsp	freshly cracked black peppercorns (see Tips, left)	15 mL

1. Rinse chicken and pat dry.

2. In a large saucepan, stir together yogurt, cornstarch, ginger, garlic, chilies and salt. Add chicken and mix well. Marinate for 30 minutes at room temperature.

3. Cover and bring to a boil over medium heat. Reduce heat and simmer, shaking pan occasionally and turning pieces once to ensure even cooking, for 30 to 35 minutes. (Yogurt will curdle. Don't worry as it will be fine when dish is finished.) If there is too much liquid, increase heat and leave uncovered.

4. Reduce heat, shaking pan occasionally, until there is about 1 cup (250 mL) liquid and chicken is tender and no longer pink inside. Stir gently to loosen chicken from bottom of pan. Scatter cilantro over top.

5. In a small saucepan, heat oil over medium heat. Add peppercorns and cook until sizzling, about 1 minute. Pour over chicken and mix gently. Remove from heat. Cover and let stand for 5 minutes before serving.

Ginger Chili Chicken

Serves 8

The astonishing flavors of this simple dish will amaze you. Use the freshest ginger you can find, because the juice will greatly enhance the taste. A "dry" dish (see Tips, below), this recipe is best served with a traditional Indian bread accompanied by raita or plain yogurt.

❋

TIPS

Most Indian meals have a "wet" dish or two balanced with one or more "dry" dishes. When a wet dish, such as a soupy dal or curry, is part of the menu, a dry dish, such as this recipe, provides the textural contrast.

◆

If you prefer to use boneless thighs or breasts, adjust the cooking time so as not to overcook. I find bone-in thighs more moist, and the bone adds flavor.

12	skinless bone-in chicken thighs	12
1/2 cup	freshly squeezed lime or lemon juice	125 mL
2 1/2 tsp	freshly ground black pepper	12 mL
1 1/2 tsp	mustard powder	7 mL
2 tsp	salt or to taste	10 mL
3 tbsp	vegetable oil	45 mL
1/2 cup	julienne peeled gingerroot	125 mL
6 to 8	green chilies, preferably serranos, julienned	6 to 8
	Lemon or lime slices, for garnish	
1	sprig cilantro, for garnish	1

1. Rinse chicken and pat dry.

2. In a large bowl, combine lime juice, pepper, mustard powder and salt. Add chicken and mix well. Marinate at room temperature for 30 minutes.

3. In a large skillet with a tight-fitting lid, heat oil over medium-high heat. Sauté ginger and chilies until almost crisp, about 2 minutes.

4. Add chicken with marinade. Reduce heat to medium and brown for 4 to 5 minutes per side. Add 2 tbsp (25 mL) water and cover. Reduce heat to medium-low and simmer, turning once, until chicken is no longer pink inside, about 30 minutes. Shake skillet periodically to prevent sticking, adding 1 or 2 tbsp (15 to 25 mL) water if necessary. Garnish with lime slices and cilantro.

Three-Spice Chicken with Potatoes

Serves 8

This is one of my favorite recipes because you get powerful flavors with very little effort. The freshly toasted and pounded spices are a key factor in its success and worth the extra few minutes involved. If doubling the recipe, make it in two batches.

Tip

A quick way to seed cardamoms is to put the whole pods into a spice grinder or blender jar. With a few on/off pulse motions the skins will come loose. Remove and discard skins.

6	medium potatoes	6
16	skinless boneless chicken thighs, about 4 lbs (2 kg)	16
1/4 cup	vegetable oil	50 mL
5 tbsp	coriander seeds, freshly toasted and powdered in spice grinder (to yield about 1/4 cup/50 mL powder) (see Tips, page 74)	60 mL
1/4 cup	cardamom seeds, coarsely pounded (see Tip, left)	50 mL
1 tbsp	black peppercorns, coarsely pounded	15 mL
1 1/4 tsp	salt or to taste	6 mL
	Cherry tomatoes, halved, for garnish	

1. In a saucepan of boiling water, cook whole potatoes with skins on until tender, 20 to 25 minutes. Drain. When cool enough to handle, peel and cut into quarters. Set aside.
2. Rinse chicken and pat dry.
3. In a large wok or saucepan with a tight-fitting lid, heat oil over medium-high heat. Add chicken.
4. Mix together coriander powder, cardamom seeds, pepper and salt. Sprinkle evenly over chicken. Reduce heat to medium. Cover and cook, shaking pan occasionally to prevent sticking. Do not stir. (There will be a fair amount of liquid from the chicken as it cooks.) After 8 to 10 minutes, when there is no more liquid, add potatoes. Brown chicken and potatoes gently. If chicken is not cooked, add 2 to 3 tbsp (25 to 45 mL) water. Cover and cook over low heat until potatoes are tender and chicken is no longer pink inside, 10 to 12 minutes.
5. *To serve:* Mound on platter and garnish with halved cherry tomatoes.

Masala-Coated
Baked Chicken

This recipe comes from John, a chef who cooked for my husband's family for about 40 years. His dishes, which he prepared for princes and maharajas, were among the most elaborate I have eaten. He always had a young assistant, or masalchi, whose primary function was to grind fresh spices and pastes for every dish. John was a true master, creating dishes that still live in the memory of our everyday family meals.

❋

TIP

To test for doneness, insert tip of paring knife into thickest part of thigh: chicken juices should run clear.

◆ *Preheat oven to 350°F (180°C)*
◆ *Shallow baking dish, lined with foil and lightly oiled*

¼ cup	poppy seeds	50 mL
¼ cup	coriander powder	50 mL
2	sticks cinnamon, each about 3 inches (7.5 cm) long	2
16	whole cloves	16
12	green cardamom pods, peeled and seeded	12
6	whole dried red chilies, seeds removed	6
1 tsp	black peppercorns	5 mL
1 tsp	paprika	5 mL
2 tbsp	minced peeled gingerroot	25 mL
2 tbsp	minced garlic	25 mL
1 tbsp	turmeric	15 mL
3 tbsp	vegetable oil	45 mL
3 cups	packed finely chopped onions (about 3)	750 mL
3 cups	finely chopped tomatoes	750 mL
2 tsp	salt or to taste	10 mL
3 tbsp	tomato paste	45 mL
12	skinless bone-in chicken thighs, about 4 lbs (2 kg)	12
	Lemon slices, for garnish	
	Finely chopped cilantro, for garnish	

1. In a spice grinder, combine poppy seeds, coriander powder, cinnamon, cloves, cardamom, chilies, peppercorns and paprika. Grind as fine as possible. Place in a bowl and mix with ginger, garlic and turmeric. Moisten with just enough water to make a smooth paste, about 3 tbsp (45 mL). Set masala paste aside.

2. In a large saucepan, heat oil over medium–high heat. Sauté onions until beginning to color, 6 to 8 minutes. Reduce heat to medium and sauté until dark brown, 12 to 15 minutes.

3. Reduce heat to medium-low and add masala paste. Sauté, stirring often and drizzling with 1 tbsp (15 mL) water at a time to prevent burning, until darker in color, 4 to 5 minutes.

4. Stir in tomatoes. Add salt and mix well. Increase heat to medium and cook until tomatoes are soft and mushy, 6 to 8 minutes. Mash with back of spoon. Mix in tomato paste.

5. Rinse chicken and pat dry. Add to masala paste. Increase heat to medium-high. When chicken is cooking briskly, reduce heat to medium and cook for 10 to 12 minutes longer. Remove chicken from gravy and set aside.

6. If gravy is not thick enough to thickly coat chicken, reduce until no liquid remains and mixture (masala) forms a mass.

7. Coat chicken pieces with masala and arrange in prepared baking dish. Bake in preheated oven until chicken is no longer pink inside, 30 to 35 minutes.

8. Garnish with lemon slices and cilantro and serve with Indian bread.

Preeti's Brown Onion Chicken

Rich-tasting but amazingly healthy, this dish was created by my daughter-in-law, Preeti, who is a fabulous creative cook. The key to success here is taking the time to caramelize the onions for the deep, rich flavor.

TIP

Red chilies and whole spices should be removed before serving. They are used for flavor only, and the chilies are too fiery to eat.

12	skinless bone-in chicken thighs, about 4 lbs (2 kg)	12
1/4 cup	vegetable oil, divided	50 mL
2 cups	chopped onions (about 1 1/2)	500 mL
2 cups	plain nonfat yogurt, at room temperature	500 mL
2 tsp	cornstarch	10 mL
1 tsp	minced garlic	5 mL
1/2 tsp	minced peeled gingerroot	2 mL
3/4 tsp	black cumin (shah jeera)	4 mL
1/2 tsp	cumin seeds	2 mL
4	bay leaves	4
6	green cardamom pods, cracked open	6
5	whole cloves	5
1	stick cinnamon, about 1 inch (2.5 cm) long	1
3	whole dried red chilies, seeds removed if desired (see Tip, left)	3
2 tsp	salt or to taste	10 mL
1 cup	cilantro, chopped, divided	250 mL

1. Rinse chicken and pat dry.

2. In a large saucepan with a tight-fitting lid, heat 2 tbsp (25 mL) of the oil over medium-high heat. Sauté onions until beginning to color, 4 to 5 minutes. Reduce heat to medium and sauté until dark brown, 15 to 20 minutes longer.

3. Transfer onions to a blender. Stir yogurt to a creamy consistency and mix in cornstarch. Add 1 cup (250 mL) of the yogurt mixture to blender. Blend until smooth. Stir back into remaining yogurt. Set aside.

4. In the same saucepan, heat remaining oil over medium heat. Stir in garlic and ginger. Sauté for 30 seconds. Add black cumin, cumin seeds, bay leaves, cardamom pods, cloves, cinnamon and chilies. Sauté for 1 minute.

5. Increase heat to medium–high. Add chicken and salt and brown, 6 to 8 minutes per side.

6. Add yogurt mixture and half of the cilantro. Cover and bring to a boil. Reduce heat to low and simmer until chicken is no longer pink inside and gravy is thick, about 30 minutes. Discard bay leaves, cloves, cinnamon stick and chilies, if desired. Fold in remaining cilantro just before serving.

Saagwalla Murg
Chicken with Aromatic Puréed Spinach

	Serves 8	

Chicken or lamb cooked with spinach is a north Indian favorite that appears on most restaurant menus. I like the flavor and texture of the creamy spinach complementing the chicken.

12	skinless bone-in chicken thighs, about 4 lbs (2 kg)	12
¼ cup	freshly squeezed lemon juice	50 mL
2 tbsp	vegetable oil	25 mL
2 cups	finely sliced onions (about 1½)	500 mL
1 tbsp	minced green chilies, preferably serranos	15 mL
1 tsp	minced peeled gingerroot	5 mL
1 tsp	minced garlic	5 mL
2 tsp	coriander powder	10 mL
1 tsp	cumin powder	5 mL
½ tsp	turmeric	2 mL
½ tsp	cayenne pepper	2 mL
1 cup	chopped tomatoes	250 mL
2 tsp	salt or to taste	10 mL
2	packages (each 10 oz/300 g) frozen spinach, thawed	2
	Juice of 1 lime or lemon	

1. Rinse chicken and pat dry. Marinate in lemon juice for 20 to 30 minutes.

2. Meanwhile, in a large saucepan, heat oil over medium-high heat. Sauté onions until beginning to color, 4 to 5 minutes. Reduce heat to medium and sauté until golden, 12 to 14 minutes longer. Stir in chilies, ginger and garlic. Sauté for 2 minutes.

3. Add coriander, cumin, turmeric and cayenne pepper. Reduce heat to low and sauté for 2 minutes.

4. Place chicken on top of masala. Scatter tomatoes over top of chicken. Sprinkle with salt. Cover and cook over low heat for 10 minutes.

5. Turn chicken over. Mix with masala, scraping bottom of pan. Add 2 tbsp (25 mL) water if necessary to deglaze. Cover and cook for 10 minutes longer.

6. Meanwhile, in a blender, purée spinach with 1½ cups (375 mL) water. Pour into chicken and mix. Cover and simmer until gravy is thick and chicken is no longer pink inside, 10 to 15 minutes.

7. Remove from heat and stir in lime juice. Serve with rice or an Indian bread.

Sindhi Chicken Curry

This is the quintessential north Indian-style chicken curry with onion and tomato-based gravy. It is a simple home-style version, but the amazing flavors and bright, appetizing color make it suitable for company as well.

❄

TIP

This dish freezes very well in an airtight container for up to 4 months. Thaw in refrigerator overnight. Reheat on low heat. Sprinkle with garam masala and cumin powder. Cover and let stand for 2 to 3 minutes to allow the aroma of the spices to infuse the curry. Transfer to a serving dish and sprinkle with chopped cilantro before serving.

12	skinless bone-in chicken thighs, about 4 lbs (2 kg)	12
1 cup	plain nonfat yogurt, at room temperature	250 mL
1 tsp	cornstarch	5 mL
2 tbsp	vegetable oil	25 mL
2 cups	finely chopped onions (about 1 1/2)	500 mL
1 tbsp	minced peeled gingerroot	15 mL
1 tbsp	minced garlic	15 mL
1 tbsp	minced green chilies, preferably serranos	15 mL
1 tbsp	coriander powder	15 mL
1 1/2 tsp	cumin powder	7 mL
3/4 tsp	turmeric	4 mL
3/4 tsp	cayenne pepper	4 mL
1	can (28 oz/796 mL) tomatoes, chopped, including juice	1
1/2 cup	cilantro, chopped	125 mL
2 tsp	salt or to taste	10 mL
1 1/2 tsp	garam masala	7 mL
1/4 cup	cilantro, chopped, divided	50 mL

1. Rinse chicken and pat dry.

2. Stir together yogurt and cornstarch until smooth. Set aside.

3. In a large saucepan with a tight-fitting lid, heat oil over medium–high heat. Add onions and sauté until beginning to color, 6 to 8 minutes. Reduce heat to medium and sauté until dark golden, 10 to 12 minutes longer.

4. Stir in ginger, garlic and chilies. Sauté for 2 minutes. Increase heat to medium–high. Add chicken and brown well, 6 to 8 minutes.

5. Reduce heat to medium. Add coriander, cumin, turmeric and cayenne pepper. Mix well and cook for 2 to 3 minutes.

6. Add tomatoes, yogurt mixture, $\frac{1}{2}$ cup (125 mL) cilantro and salt. Mix well. Cover and bring to a boil.

7. Reduce heat to low and simmer until chicken is no longer pink inside, about 25 minutes.

8. Remove from heat. Stir in garam masala and 3 tbsp (45 mL) cilantro.

9. Garnish with remaining cilantro before serving. Serve with rice or an Indian bread.

Chicken in
Cashew Saffron Gravy

The delicious gravy in this dish is versatile and easy to prepare. Use it for shrimp, fish or any other type of seafood. It can be prepared ahead and refrigerated for several days, or frozen for up to three months.

❋

TIPS

Thighs and drumsticks work best in this recipe because they do not dry out as chicken breast does when braised.

◆

Masala paste can be made a day ahead and refrigerated.

◆

Crisp fried onions are available in Asian and Middle Eastern markets or make your own (see page 22). Store the remainder in an airtight container in the refrigerator for up to 1 year.

1 tsp	saffron	5 mL
MASALA PASTE		
4 cups	chopped tomatoes	1 L
1½ cups	crisp fried onions (birishta) (see Tips, left)	375 mL
½ cup	raw cashews	125 mL
2	green chilies, preferably serranos	2
1	piece (1 inch/2.5 cm) peeled gingerroot	1
4 to 5	cloves garlic	4 to 5
½ cup	cilantro, chopped	125 mL
1 tbsp	cayenne pepper or to taste	15 mL
3 tbsp	vegetable oil	45 mL
CHICKEN		
12	skinless bone-in chicken thighs, or thighs and drumsticks, about 4 lbs (2 kg)	12
2 tsp	salt or to taste	10 mL
1 tsp	garam masala	5 mL
1 tsp	cardamom powder	5 mL
1 cup	cilantro, chopped	250 mL

1. Soak saffron in ½ cup (125 mL) very hot water. Set aside.

2. *Masala Paste:* In a blender, combine tomatoes, fried onions, cashews, chilies, ginger, garlic, ½ cup (125 mL) cilantro and cayenne. Blend in ½ to ¾ cup (125 to 175 mL) water, a little at a time, to make a very creamy paste (a little thicker than consistency of cake batter).

3. In a large saucepan, heat oil over medium heat. Pour in masala paste. Stir-fry until masala is darker and aromatic, 5 to 6 minutes. If it begins to stick to bottom of pan, deglaze with 1 to 2 tbsp (15 to 25 mL) water. Continue until masala is well browned. Move to side of pan.

4. *Chicken:* Rinse chicken and pat dry. Arrange in single layer in saucepan. Add salt. Spoon masala on top. Cook, uncovered, for about 8 minutes. Turn pieces over and cook for 4 minutes longer. Stir to mix well. Reduce heat to low and cook, covered, for about 20 minutes longer.

5. Add garam masala, reserved saffron water and cardamom powder. Cover and cook, stirring occasionally, until chicken is tender and no longer pink inside, about 20 minutes. If curry looks too thick, dilute with a little hot water to desired consistency. Mix well and simmer for 2 to 3 minutes longer.

6. Remove from heat. Stir in ¾ cup (175 mL) of the cilantro. Serve hot over rice or with an Indian bread. Garnish with remaining cilantro.

Khubani Murg

Chicken with Dried Apricots

Serves 8

This a classic dish from the north. Apricots were introduced by the Moghuls, Muslim rulers who enriched India's art, architecture and cuisine and whose influence on north Indian food is indelible. Their legacy, Moghlai food, remains the most popular of all the regional cuisines. The apricots provide a pleasing sweet contrast to the spices, resulting in a glorious complexity of flavors and textures.

❋

TIP

The apricots used in this dish are small, tan colored and fairly hard, with a stone. They are usually available in Indian stores. Remove stones with the tip of a paring knife after soaking. You can substitute regular dried apricots.

1/2 tsp	saffron threads	2 mL
12	skinless bone-in chicken thighs, or thighs and drumsticks, about 4 lbs (2 kg)	12
2 tbsp	vegetable oil	25 mL
4 cups	finely sliced onions (about 3)	1 L
1 1/2 tbsp	minced peeled gingerroot	22 mL
1 1/2 tbsp	minced garlic	22 mL
1 tbsp	minced green chilies, preferably serranos	15 mL
1	stick cinnamon, about 4 inches (10 cm) long	1
4	green cardamom pods, cracked open	4
2 tsp	salt or to taste	10 mL
1	can (14 oz/398 mL) tomatoes, puréed with liquid	1
8 oz	dried apricots, stones removed (see Tip, left)	250 g

1. Soak saffron in 1/4 cup (50 mL) very hot water. Set aside.

2. Rinse chicken and pat dry. Set aside.

3. In a large saucepan, heat oil over medium-high heat. Sauté onions until beginning to color, 6 to 8 minutes. Reduce heat to medium and sauté until golden, 10 to 12 minutes longer.

4. Stir in ginger, garlic and chilies. Sauté for 5 minutes.

5. Increase heat to medium-high. Add chicken, cinnamon, cardamom pods and salt. Sauté until browned, 8 to 10 minutes per side.

6. Add tomatoes and mix well. Cover and bring to a boil. Reduce heat to low and simmer until chicken is tender and no longer pink inside, about 30 minutes.

7. Add apricots and reserved saffron water. Simmer for 10 minutes. Discard cinnamon stick. Serve with rice or an Indian bread.

Keema Matar
Spiced Ground Beef with Peas

Ground meat is undoubtedly the most popular form of red meat for Indians because of its versatility. This recipe can be made with or without peas and is a basic form of keema. Do not skimp on the onions because they provide flavor and thicken the dish. It is very important to brown the onions until they are caramelized.

❋

TIP

Keema can be served over halved hamburger buns like a sloppy Joe, over rice or with any Indian bread. I like to make a big pot of keema and freeze it in small containers to use as an ingredient in other dishes, such as stuffed peppers. Do not cook more than 3 lbs (1.5 kg) ground meat at a time as it will be difficult to brown.

2 tbsp	vegetable oil	25 mL
2 lbs	onions, chopped (about 7 cups/1.75 L)	1 kg
2 lbs	lean ground beef or lamb	1 kg
1½ tbsp	minced peeled gingerroot	22 mL
1 tbsp	minced garlic	15 mL
3 to 4 tsp	chopped green chilies, preferably serranos	15 to 20 mL
1 tbsp	coriander powder	15 mL
1½ tsp	cumin powder	22 mL
¾ tsp	cayenne pepper	4 mL
¾ tsp	turmeric	4 mL
1½ tsp	salt or to taste	7 mL
1	can (28 oz/796 mL) chopped tomatoes, including juice	1
1	package (10 oz/300 g) frozen peas	1
1 tsp	garam masala	5 mL
⅓ cup	cilantro, chopped	75 mL

1. In a large saucepan, heat oil over medium-high heat. Sauté onions until beginning to color, 10 to 12 minutes. Reduce heat to medium and sauté until dark brown, 25 to 30 minutes longer, stirring frequently to prevent sticking to pan. If necessary, deglaze periodically with 2 tbsp (25 mL) water.

2. Add ground beef, ginger, garlic and chilies. Brown well, stirring frequently, 15 to 20 minutes. Continue to deglaze with water as necessary.

3. Reduce heat to medium-low. Add coriander, cumin, cayenne pepper, turmeric and salt. Mix well. Sauté, stirring continuously, for 3 to 4 minutes.

4. Add tomatoes with juice and mix well. Cover and cook for 10 minutes.

5. Add peas and simmer for 10 to 15 minutes. Remove from heat and sprinkle with garam masala. Cover and let stand for 5 minutes. Stir mixture. Garnish with cilantro just before serving.

Gena's Kababs

**Makes
12 to 14 kababs**

I am always on a quest for authentic, home-style recipes when I travel to India. On one of my many visits, I was fortunate enough to spend an afternoon in the kitchen of a legendary cook who was a friend of my husband's family. This treasured recipe is one she cooked while I watched and made notes.

❋

TIPS

Crisp fried onions can be stored, tightly sealed, in the refrigerator for up to 1 year.

◆

Crush mustard seeds with a mortar and pestle.

◆

In Indian cooking, it is not always necessary to thread kababs. In this recipe, they are cooked in a nonstick skillet.

1 cup	plain nonfat yogurt, at room temperature	250 mL
1 tsp	cornstarch	5 mL
10 to 12	green onions, coarsely chopped	10 to 12
1	piece (1 inch/2.5 cm) peeled gingerroot, cut into chunks	1
2 to 3	green chilies, preferably serranos, coarsely chopped	2 to 3
1/4 cup	cilantro leaves	50 mL
1 lb	lean ground beef or lamb	500 g
1/2 cup	crisp fried onions (birishta) (see Tips, left and on page 86)	125 mL
2 tsp	coriander powder	10 mL
1 tsp	cumin powder	5 mL
1 tsp	crushed mustard seeds (see Tips, left)	5 mL
1 1/2 tsp	salt or to taste	7 mL
1 tbsp	vegetable oil	15 mL
1 1/2 cups	finely chopped tomatoes	375 mL

1. Stir together yogurt and cornstarch until smooth. Set aside.

2. In a food processor, chop green onions, ginger, chilies and cilantro leaves.

3. Add ground beef, crisp fried onions, coriander, cumin, mustard seeds and salt. Process until well mixed, about 1 minute.

4. Roll mixture into 12 to 14 kababs, each about 3 inches by 3/4 inch (7.5 by 2 cm).

5. Arrange kababs in a single layer in a nonstick skillet over medium-high heat. Pour yogurt mixture over top. Cook, uncovered, until all moisture is absorbed, shaking pan occasionally and rotating kababs if necessary, 10 to 12 minutes.

6. Drizzle oil around edge of skillet and brown kababs, about 5 minutes. Add tomatoes and 1/2 cup (125 mL) water. Reduce heat to medium-low. Cover and simmer until tomatoes are softened and very thick gravy coats kababs, 6 to 8 minutes.

Lamb with Fennel and Nigella

This recipe came from another good friend who is an outstanding cook. I changed the original name, Pickled Meat, because the two signature spices that are synonymous with pickles just do not translate well in the culinary milieu in North America. The new name is, I feel, far more descriptive of this wonderful dish.

❋

2 cups	coarsely chopped onions (about 1 ½)	500 mL
1 ½ tbsp	minced peeled gingerroot	22 mL
1 ½ tbsp	minced garlic	22 mL
¾ cup	cider vinegar	175 mL
2 lbs	boneless lamb, cut into bite-size pieces, or stewing beef	1 kg
1 ½ tsp	cayenne pepper	7 mL
2 tsp	salt or to taste	10 mL
2 tbsp	vegetable oil	25 mL
3 tbsp	fennel seeds, coarsely ground (saunf)	45 mL
2 tsp	nigella seeds (kalaunji)	10 mL
	Sliced tomatoes and lemon wedges, for garnish	

1. In a food processor or blender, purée onions.

2. In a large saucepan, stir together puréed onions, ginger, garlic and vinegar. Add lamb. Mix well. Marinate in refrigerator for 1 hour.

3. Cover saucepan and bring to a boil over high heat. Reduce heat to medium-low and simmer for 20 minutes.

4. Stir in cayenne pepper and salt. Continue to cook until meat is tender and liquid is almost evaporated, 20 to 25 minutes. (If meat is cooked and there is still too much liquid, uncover and increase heat to evaporate excess.) Stir carefully, without breaking up meat, and do not allow masala to stick to bottom of pan.

5. In a small saucepan, heat oil over medium heat until very hot. Add fennel and nigella seeds. Sauté until seeds are aromatic, about 30 seconds. Pour over meat and mix gently. Mound mixture on a platter and serve garnished with sliced tomatoes and lemon wedges.

Kofta Curry
Meatball Curry

Serves 6

The koftas (meatballs) will be soft and succulent because no egg is used to bind the mixture. The unique technique creates koftas that are firm but not hard and that absorb flavors well. They make a wonderful meatball sandwich.

❋

KOFTAS

2 lbs	lean ground beef or lamb	1 kg
1/2 cup	chopped onion	125 mL
3 tbsp	cilantro, chopped	45 mL
2 tsp	minced green chilies, preferably serranos	10 mL
1 tsp	minced peeled gingerroot	5 mL
1 tsp	minced garlic	5 mL
1 1/2 tsp	coriander powder	7 mL
1 tsp	garam masala	5 mL
3/4 tsp	cumin powder	4 mL
1/2 tsp	cayenne pepper	2 mL
1 tsp	salt or to taste	5 mL

CURRY

2 tbsp	vegetable oil	25 mL
1 1/2 cups	chopped onions	375 mL
1 tbsp	minced peeled gingerroot	15 mL
1 tbsp	minced garlic	15 mL
1 tbsp	minced green chilies, preferably serranos	15 mL
2 tsp	coriander powder	10 mL
1 tsp	cumin powder	5 mL
1/2 tsp	turmeric	2 mL
1/2 tsp	cayenne pepper	2 mL
1	can (28 oz/796 mL) tomatoes, puréed with juice	1
1/4 cup	cilantro, chopped	50 mL
1 1/2 tsp	salt or to taste	7 mL
1 tsp	garam masala	5 mL
2 tbsp	cilantro, chopped, for garnish	25 mL

1. *Koftas:* In a bowl, combine ground beef, onion, cilantro, chilies, ginger, garlic, coriander powder, garam masala, cumin, cayenne pepper and salt. Mix by hand. (Do not use a food processor.) Form into 30 to 35 walnut-size balls. Use a light touch; do not compact or the meatballs will be too hard. Place on baking sheet. Set aside.

TIP

The gravy may appear to be too soupy. This is the way Indians like it, because it is spooned on top of rice and absorbed. If served with an Indian bread, the bread is used to dunk in the gravy — considered by some to be the best part of the dish. If you prefer, reduce to desired amount by simmering uncovered.

2. *Curry:* In a large deep skillet with a tight–fitting lid, heat oil over medium-high heat. Sauté onions until beginning to color, 6 to 8 minutes. Reduce heat to medium and sauté until browned, 8 to 10 minutes longer. Pour in 1 cup (250 mL) water.

3. Place baking sheet with meatballs on top of saucepan, making sure the pan is covered completely. Reduce heat to low and simmer until onions are very soft, 8 to 10 minutes, or until water has evaporated. The meatballs will "set" because of the steam from the pan, which will prevent them from breaking while browning.

4. When onions are soft and there is no more liquid in the pan, carefully lift meatballs from baking sheet and arrange on top of onions, turning them bottom side up when transferring from baking sheet.

5. Cover pan to allow meatballs to set, 1 to 2 minutes. Uncover, increase heat to medium-low and cook until meatballs are firm enough to turn gently with spoon and all the meat juices have been absorbed, 6 to 8 minutes. Gently stir meatballs to brown, taking care not to break them.

6. Scatter ginger, garlic, chilies, coriander, cumin, turmeric and cayenne pepper over top. Reduce heat to low and continue to brown for 2 minutes longer. If masala sticks to pan, add 2 tbsp (25 mL) water to deglaze and mix well.

7. Stir in tomatoes, ¼ cup (50 mL) cilantro and salt. Increase heat to medium. Cover and return to a gentle boil. Reduce heat to low and simmer, covered, stirring occasionally, until gravy is thick, 20 to 30 minutes.

8. Remove from heat and sprinkle garam masala over top. Cover and let stand for 5 minutes. Stir mixture. Garnish with 2 tbsp (25 mL) cilantro before serving. Serve with rice or an Indian bread.

North Indian–Style Lamb Curry on Bread

Serves 8		

This substantial dish is popular for brunch, but I have also served it at the end of a cocktail party when party-goers were tired of finger foods.

TIP

Gravy should be slightly runny to soften the bread. If it has cooked down too much, add a little hot water and simmer to incorporate.

1 cup	plain nonfat yogurt, at room temperature	250 mL
1 tsp	cornstarch	5 mL
2 tbsp	vegetable oil	25 mL
4 cups	finely chopped onions (3 to 4)	1 L
4 tsp	minced peeled gingerroot	20 mL
4 tsp	minced garlic	20 mL
1 tbsp	minced green chilies, preferably serranos	15 mL
3 lbs	boneless leg of lamb, cut into bite-size pieces	1.5 kg
4 tsp	coriander powder	20 mL
2 tsp	cumin powder	10 mL
¾ tsp	turmeric	4 mL
½ tsp	cayenne pepper	2 mL
2 tsp	salt or to taste	10 mL
2	can (each 28 oz/796 mL) diced tomatoes	2
1 tsp	garam masala	5 mL
¼ cup	cilantro, chopped	50 mL
1	loaf soft French bread, sliced 1 inch (2.5 cm) thick	1
	Thin slices onions or green onions, for garnish	
3 tbsp	cilantro, chopped, for garnish	45 mL
	Juice of ½ lime or lemon	

1. Stir together yogurt and cornstarch until smooth. Set aside.

2. In a large saucepan, heat oil over medium–high heat. Sauté onions until beginning to color, 6 to 8 minutes. Reduce heat to medium and sauté until browned, 15 to 20 minutes longer.

3. Stir in ginger, garlic and chilies. Sauté for 3 to 4 minutes. Increase heat to medium–high. Add lamb and brown until meat and onions are a dark rich brown, 10 to 15 minutes. Add water, 1 tbsp (15 mL) at a time, if necessary to prevent burning.

4. Add coriander, cumin, turmeric, cayenne pepper and salt. Reduce heat to medium. Sauté for 3 to 4 minutes. Add tomatoes and yogurt mixture and return to a boil.

5. Reduce heat to maintain a gentle boil. Cover and cook, stirring occasionally, until meat is tender, about 1 hour. Remove from heat. Sprinkle with garam masala and ¼ cup (50 mL) cilantro. There should be a lot of gravy.

6. *To serve:* Arrange bread in single layer on a large serving platter. Top with lamb and spoon gravy evenly over top to soak into bread. (Assemble 10 minutes before serving to allow bread to soak up gravy.) Garnish with onions and 3 tbsp (45 mL) cilantro. Sprinkle with lime juice.

Cardamom-Scented Lamb

Serves 8		

This is a classic Sindhi dish that was cooked frequently in my home because my father loved it. Its soupy, lightly spiced consistency is considered very nourishing. Traditionally, it is spooned over a chapati (whole wheat flatbread) to completely soak and soften it.

❁

TIP

The spinach is used for flavor and as a thickener. It will be barely visible.

2 tbsp	vegetable oil	25 mL
¼ cup	cardamom seeds, removed from pods and crushed	50 mL
2 lbs	boneless lamb, cut into bite-size pieces	1 kg
1 lb	fresh spinach, washed and chopped (about 4 cups/1 L)	500 g
1 cup	chopped tomatoes	250 mL
2 tsp	coriander powder	10 mL
1½ tsp	salt or to taste	7 mL
½ tsp	freshly ground black pepper	2 mL
1½ tbsp	all-purpose flour	22 mL

1. In a large saucepan, heat oil over medium–high heat. Stir in cardamom seeds and sauté until fragrant, about 1 minute.

2. Add lamb and spinach. Reduce heat to medium. Cover and cook until spinach loses all moisture, 4 to 5 minutes. Uncover and brown lamb for 8 to 10 minutes.

3. Add tomatoes and cook until moisture is evaporated, 10 minutes longer.

4. Sprinkle with coriander, salt and pepper. Mix well and brown for 2 minutes longer.

5. Pour in 2 cups (500 mL) water. Bring to a boil over medium–high heat. Reduce heat to low. Cover and simmer until lamb is tender, 45 minutes to 1 hour.

6. Stir flour with 4 tbsp (60 mL) water to make a smooth paste. Gradually pour over lamb, stirring continuously. When thickened, remove from heat. Serve with Indian bread.

Pork Vindaloo (page 102)

Overleaf: Coconut Chutney–Coated Fish Parcels (page 118)

Sial Gosht
Lamb Braised in Yogurt, Tomatoes and Onions

Serves 8		

Another favorite from the state of Sind, this dish was prepared often in our home. We used goat (cabrito), but lamb is just as good. Light on the stomach yet full of flavor, the meat is juicy and very, very tender, thanks to slow cooking.

❋

1 cup	plain nonfat yogurt, at room temperature	250 mL
1 tsp	cornstarch	5 mL
2 lbs	boneless lamb, cut into bite-size pieces	1 kg
1½ cups	minced onions	375 mL
1 cup	chopped tomatoes	250 mL
⅓ cup	cilantro, chopped	75 mL
1½ tbsp	minced peeled gingerroot	22 mL
1 tbsp	minced garlic	15 mL
1 tbsp	minced green chilies, preferably serranos	15 mL
1 tbsp	coriander powder	15 mL
1½ tsp	cumin powder	7 mL
¾ tsp	cayenne pepper	4 mL
¾ tsp	turmeric	4 mL
2 tsp	salt or to taste	10 mL
2 tbsp	vegetable oil	25 mL
1 tsp	garam masala	5 mL
3 tbsp	cilantro, chopped, for garnish	45 mL

1. Stir yogurt to a creamy consistency. Add cornstarch and stir together.

2. In a saucepan, combine lamb, onions, tomatoes, ⅓ cup (75 mL) cilantro, ginger, garlic, chilies, coriander powder, cumin, cayenne pepper, turmeric, salt, yogurt mixture and oil. Mix well, preferably with your hands. Marinate for 30 minutes at room temperature.

3. Cover and bring to a boil over medium–high heat. Reduce heat to maintain a gentle boil. Cook, stirring occasionally, until meat is fork–tender, about 1 hour. If too much liquid remains after meat is cooked, uncover, increase heat and reduce until gravy is thickened.

4. Remove from heat and sprinkle with garam masala. Cover and let stand for 5 minutes for flavors to permeate. Stir mixture. Garnish with 3 tbsp (45 mL) cilantro and serve with rice or an Indian bread.

Goa Seafood Curry (page 110)

Dry-Fried Lamb with Coconut Slices

A friend from Kerala shared this recipe from her family. It is typical of the dishes from the area, though it would have been made with goat, of course. Coconut is widely used in Kerala since coconut palms are abundant throughout the state.

❋

TIP

To obtain fresh coconut slices, start with a coconut that feels heavy and has liquid sloshing around inside. Break open with a hammer and, with knife, pry meat out of shell. Using a vegetable peeler or sharp paring knife, remove brown skin. Cut coconut meat into slices. Alternatively, substitute ⅓ cup (75 mL) unsweetened shredded coconut, toasted.

2 lbs	boneless lamb, preferably from the leg, cut into 1½-inch (4 cm) pieces	1 kg
2 tsp	salt or to taste, divided	10 mL
15 to 20	slices fresh coconut, very thinly sliced (about 1 inch/2.5 cm long) (see Tip, left)	15 to 20
¼ cup	vegetable oil	50 mL
1 cup	finely sliced onion (about 1)	250 mL
3	green chilies, preferably serranos, slivered	3
2 tsp	minced peeled gingerroot	10 mL
2 tsp	minced garlic	10 mL
2 tsp	Asian red chili paste (sambal olek)	10 mL
2 tbsp	coriander powder	25 mL
18 to 20	fresh curry leaves (optional)	18 to 20
2 cups	chopped tomatoes	500 mL
1 tsp	fennel seeds, powdered	5 mL

1. Place lamb in a pan with 1½ tsp (7 mL) of the salt and just enough water to cover. Bring to a boil over medium-high heat. Remove scum. Reduce heat to medium-low. Cover and cook, maintaining a gentle boil, until meat is tender and there is no water remaining, about 1 hour.

2. Meanwhile, in a skillet over medium-low heat, toast coconut slices, turning to cook evenly, until golden, 3 to 4 minutes. Set aside.

3. In a saucepan, heat oil over medium-high heat. Sauté onion until golden, 4 to 5 minutes.

4. Stir in chilies, ginger and garlic. Stir-fry for 1 minute. Add red chili paste, coriander and curry leaves, if using. Stir-fry for 2 minutes.

5. Add tomatoes and remaining salt. Mix well. Reduce heat to medium-low. Cover and cook until tomatoes are softened, 4 to 5 minutes. Mash with back of spoon.

6. Stir in lamb, taking care not to break up pieces. Brown in masala for 5 to 8 minutes.

7. Sprinkle with powdered fennel. Garnish with toasted coconut slices. Serve with an Indian bread.

Rogan Josh
Curried Lamb

Serves 8		

This classic dish from Kashmir features lamb, which is favored there over goat, the meat of choice in most of India. Rogan Josh is a popular item on restaurant menus.

2 lbs	boneless lamb, cut into bite-size pieces	1 kg
2 tsp	salt or to taste	10 mL
½ tsp	cayenne pepper	2 mL
1 cup	plain nonfat yogurt, at room temperature	250 mL
1 tsp	cornstarch	5 mL
1 tbsp	minced peeled gingerroot	15 mL
½ tsp	asafetida (hing), dissolved in 1 tbsp (15 mL) hot water	2 mL
2 tbsp	vegetable oil	25 mL
1 tsp	paprika	5 mL
½ tsp	freshly ground black pepper	2 mL
½ tsp	turmeric	2 mL
3 tbsp	cilantro, chopped	45 mL
½ tsp	garam masala	2 mL
½ tsp	ground nutmeg, preferably freshly grated	2 mL

1. Rub lamb with salt and cayenne.

2. In a large bowl, mix together yogurt, cornstarch, ginger and asafetida water. Add lamb, turning to ensure all pieces are well coated. Cover and marinate in refrigerator for at least 1 hour or for several hours.

3. In a heavy saucepan, heat oil over medium heat until very hot. Sauté paprika, pepper and turmeric, stirring briskly, for 30 seconds. Add lamb with marinade and mix well with spices. Increase heat to medium-high. Cover and bring to a boil. Immediately reduce heat to low and simmer, without stirring, for 30 minutes.

4. Sprinkle lamb with cilantro. If liquid has almost evaporated, add ½ cup (125 mL) hot water, pouring down sides of pan. Cook for 15 minutes longer and test to see if lamb is fork-tender. If necessary, add ¼ cup (50 mL) more hot water. Cover and continue cooking, adding more water if necessary, until lamb is very tender, 15 to 20 minutes longer.

5. To serve, mound lamb in a deep dish, pour remaining gravy on top and sprinkle with garam masala and nutmeg.

Oven-Braised Lamb Shanks

◆ Preheat oven to 400°F (200°C)
◆ 13-by-9 inch (3 L) baking dish

Serves 6

Rich, succulent lamb shanks are the epitome of melt-in-your-mouth lamb, the kind that Indians adore. This four-star recipe is amazingly easy and never fails to impress guests.

❖

6	lamb shanks, about 3½ to 4 lbs (1.75 to 2 kg) total	6
2 tbsp	minced peeled gingerroot	25 mL
2 tbsp	minced garlic	25 mL
¼ cup	plain nonfat yogurt	50 mL
2½ cups	thinly sliced red onions (about 1½)	625 mL
2 tbsp	vegetable oil	25 mL
1 tsp	cumin seeds	5 mL
1 tsp	black peppercorns	5 mL
4	black cardamom pods, seeds only	4
1	stick cinnamon, about 3 inches (7.5 cm) long	1
5	dried red chilies	5
2 cups	finely chopped Roma tomatoes or canned chopped tomatoes, including juice	500 mL
1 cup	crisp fried onions (birishta), crushed in food processor (see Tip, page 86)	250 mL
1½ tsp	salt	7 mL

1. Remove all fat from lamb shanks. Rinse and pat dry.

2. Stir ginger and garlic into yogurt until creamy. Coat meat with mixture. Place in a large, non-reactive pan, cover and marinate in refrigerator for at least 1 hour or for up to 24 hours. Let come to room temperature before cooking.

3. Transfer meat to baking dish. Scatter sliced onions over top. Drizzle with oil. Cover tightly and cook in preheated oven for 1 hour.

4. Meanwhile, heat a heavy skillet over medium heat for 2 minutes. Add cumin seeds, peppercorns, cardamom seeds, cinnamon and chilies. Stir periodically to evenly toast spices until aromatic, 2 to 3 minutes. Let cool. Grind to a powder in a spice grinder.

5. Combine tomatoes with spice powder, fried onions and salt.

6. Remove baking dish from oven. Reduce temperature to 350°F (180°C). Pour tomato mixture over meat. Cover again and return to oven. Cook until lamb is fork-tender and almost falling off the bone, about 1 hour.

Pork Vindaloo

Serves 4 to 6

Vindaloo, a fiery Portuguese-influenced pork dish from Goa, has become synonymous with incendiary heat. Though Goan food tends to be fiery, vindaloo has become the yardstick for the hottest of the hot. Traditionally, this curry is almost broth-like in its consistency and is eaten with lots of steamed white rice to tame the heat. However, the runny consistency does not appeal to the non-Indian palate, so it has evolved into a thickish potato-based gravy that has a familiar consistency.

Tips

Although this is traditionally a fiery dish, you can adjust the heat by controlling the amount of red chili seeds you include.

Goans use feni, a potent alcohol made from palm and cashew tree sap. The vodka is a substitute for feni, but can be omitted.

2 lbs	boneless pork, cut into bite-size pieces	1 kg
1 1/2 tsp	salt or to taste	7 mL

MARINADE

10	dried red chilies, half of the seeds removed (see Tips, left)	10
10	black peppercorns	10
10	whole cloves	10
1	stick cinnamon, about 1 inch (2.5 cm) long	1
1 tsp	cumin seeds	5 mL
1/2 tsp	mustard seeds	2 mL
1/2 tsp	granulated sugar	2 mL
10	cloves garlic	10
1	piece peeled gingerroot, 1-inch (2.5 cm) square	1
3/4 tsp	cider vinegar	4 mL
2 tbsp	vegetable oil	25 mL
3 cups	finely chopped onions (about 2)	750 mL
1/4 cup	cider vinegar	50 mL
1 cup	grated potato	250 mL
2 tbsp	vodka (optional)	25 mL

1. Rub salt into pork and set aside while preparing marinade.
2. *Marinade:* In a blender, combine chilies, peppercorns, cloves, cinnamon, cumin seeds, mustard seeds and sugar. Grind to a fine powder. Add garlic, ginger and 3/4 tsp (4 mL) vinegar. Blend to a smooth paste. Rub paste into pork. Cover and set aside in refrigerator for 2 hours.
3. In a saucepan, heat oil over medium-high heat. Sauté onions until golden, 6 to 8 minutes. Add pork and brown well, about 5 minutes.
4. Add 1/4 cup (50 mL) vinegar, potato, vodka, if using, and 1 1/4 cups (300 mL) water. Mix well. Cover and bring to a boil. Reduce heat to medium and cook until pork is tender, 20 to 25 minutes. Serve over steamed rice.

Coorg-Style Pork Curry

Serves 6

Coorg, a small region in the southern hills, where some of the best coffee is grown, is one of the two areas in India where pork dishes abound. This dish is typical of the cooking there.

1 tbsp	vegetable oil	15 mL
1 1/2 tbsp	coriander powder	22 mL
1 1/4 tsp	cayenne powder	6 mL
1/4 tsp	turmeric	1 mL
1 1/2 tsp	salt	7 mL
1 1/2 lbs	pork tenderloin, cut into 1-inch (2.5 cm) pieces	750 g
1 tsp	cumin seeds	5 mL
1 tsp	whole cloves	5 mL
1 tsp	black peppercorns or to taste	5 mL
1/2 tsp	mustard seeds	2 mL
1	large onion, chopped into chunks	1
18	cloves garlic	18
1	piece peeled gingerroot, 1/2 inch by 1 inch (1 cm x 2.5 cm), chopped into chunks	1
1 tbsp	cider vinegar	15 mL
2 tbsp	lime or lemon juice	25 mL

1. In a large saucepan, combine oil, coriander, cayenne, turmeric and salt. Add pork and marinate for 15 minutes.

2. In a spice grinder, grind cumin seeds, cloves, black peppercorns and mustard seeds into a powder.

3. In a blender, combine onion, garlic, ginger and spice powder. Purée until smooth.

4. Add onion mixture to pork. Mix well. Bring to a boil over medium-high heat. Cover pan. Reduce heat to maintain a gentle boil and cook, stirring occasionally, until pork is thoroughly cooked, 20 to 30 minutes.

5. Add vinegar. Remove from heat. Add lime juice and mix well. Serve hot with rice or an Indian bread.

Cashew and Raisin-Stuffed Pork Loin

Serves 6

Sweet raw cashews and raisins taste delicious with the hot chili and mild spices. This is an easy yet elegant dish.

TIP

The first method is easier than it sounds, and the slices are more attractive.

♦ *Preheat oven to 450°F (230°C)*

¾ cup	raw cashew pieces	175 mL
¾ cup	raisins	175 mL
1	piece peeled gingerroot, 1 inch by 1½ inches (2.5 x 4 cm), cut into pieces	1
8	large cloves garlic	8
2	green chilies, preferably serranos, cut into pieces	2
1 tbsp	coriander powder	15 mL
1½ tsp	cumin powder	7 mL
¾ tsp	salt	4 mL
¼ cup	vegetable oil	50 mL
1	boneless pork center-cut single loin roast (about 2 lbs/1 kg)	1

1. In a food processor, combine cashews, raisins, ginger, garlic, chilies, coriander, cumin and salt. Process until mixture is a coarse paste that holds together. Pour in oil and process for 30 seconds. Set aside one-third of the mixture.

2. With the short end of the pork loin facing you, work a sharp knife through the center of the pork to make a tunnel. You might have to work from both ends. Open up the tunnel with your fingers. Stuff with remaining two-thirds of the cashew mixture, packing it in and stopping ¼ inch (0.5 cm) from both ends. Cover top and sides with reserved cashew mixture, patting it on firmly.

3. Alternatively, slice pork loin horizontally almost, but not all the way through. Open into 2 flaps, like a book. Pound with a meat mallet to even thickness. Pat stuffing on one flap, leaving ¼-inch (0.5 cm) border. Cover with other flap. Tie stuffed pork with kitchen string and firmly pat reserved cashew mixture all over top and sides.

4. Roast in preheated oven for 15 minutes. Reduce temperature to 350°F (180°C) and cook for 30 minutes longer or until meat thermometer registers 160°F (70°C). Remove from oven and let stand for 10 minutes before slicing into ½-inch (1 cm) thick slices.

Coriander-Crusted Pork Chili Fry

Serves 6

Although pork is eaten by very few in India, I have found today's lean and mild-flavored pork to be particularly good with Indian spices and seasonings.

4 tsp	coriander seeds	20 mL
2 tsp	cumin seeds	10 mL
1 tsp	black peppercorns	5 mL
1 tsp	salt, divided	5 mL
1 lb	boneless top loin pork chops, well trimmed	500 g
2½ tbsp	vegetable oil, divided	32 mL
2 tsp	finely chopped garlic	10 mL
2 cups	sliced onions (about 1½)	500 mL
2 cups	sliced bell peppers, mixed colors, cut into ½-inch (1 cm) thick slices	500 mL
¾ tsp	hot pepper flakes or to taste	4 mL

1. Coarsely crush coriander, cumin and peppercorns. Mix with ½ tsp (2 mL) of the salt.

2. Cut chops into ½-inch (1 cm) wide strips and place in a large bowl. Toss with spice powder to coat strips evenly.

3. In a wok or large saucepan, heat 1½ tbsp (22 mL) of the oil over medium-high heat. Stir-fry pork for 4 minutes. Remove and set aside.

4. Reduce heat to medium. In the same wok, heat remaining oil. Stir-fry garlic for 1 minute. Add onions, bell peppers and remaining salt and stir-fry until softened, 8 to 10 minutes.

5. Increase heat to medium-high. Add pork and hot pepper flakes. Stir-fry, mixing well, for about 2 minutes longer. Serve immediately.

Fish and Seafood

THE LONG COASTLINE of India provides an exciting array of fish and seafood. Although India exports shrimp and a limited variety of fish, within the country people tend to cook the seafood of the local waters, since there are very few refrigerated trucks transporting perishables. It also means that each area has produced a vast treasure house of recipes. Bengalis make a ritual of buying fish, and most often the head of the household is entrusted with this important task. Fish is prepared daily in their homes, and Bengalis attribute their well-being to this fact. They use a lot of mustard and often cook in mustard oil. The coastal states of the south use coconut extensively, and the tiny state of Goa, influenced by more than four centuries of Portuguese rule, uses garlic and vinegar freely. Farther up the west coast, around India's famous melting pot, Mumbai (formerly known as Bombay), fresh sardines and silvery pomfret are prized. There, seafood preparations are as varied as the large number of ethnic communities.

I ate frequently with many of my classmates, sharing their home-cooked food and learning to appreciate the nuances of various cuisines. I have always enjoyed fish and all types of seafood, and most of the recipes in this chapter come from those wonderful years growing up in Mumbai, sharing the bounty of many a table.

❋ ❋ ❋

Arshi's Fish Curry

This deliciously light dish is served in a fairly thin gravy and typically eaten with chapati (an Indian whole wheat flatbread) rather than over rice. However, it is equally good with rice.

❋

3 cups	plain nonfat yogurt, at room temperature	750 mL
2 tbsp	cornstarch	25 mL
1 tbsp	vegetable oil	15 mL
1 tsp	nigella seeds (kalaunji)	5 mL
3/4 tsp	fenugreek seeds (methi)	4 mL
3 lbs	fish fillets, such as catfish, sea bass, red snapper or tilapia	1.5 kg
2 1/2 tsp	salt or to taste	12 mL
15 to 20	fresh curry leaves, chopped (optional)	15 to 20

1. Stir yogurt until it has a creamy consistency. Stir in cornstarch and set aside.

2. In a large skillet, heat oil over medium heat. Add nigella and fenugreek seeds and stir-fry for 20 to 30 seconds. Pour yogurt mixture into skillet and bring to a gentle boil over medium heat.

3. Place fish in a single layer in skillet. Sprinkle salt and curry leaves, if using, on top. Cover and return to a gentle boil. Simmer until fish flakes when tested with a fork, 6 to 8 minutes, depending on the fish used.

Red Fish Curry

Although fish curries on the west coast of India are usually made with coconut milk because it is plentiful in the area, this recipe is one of the few that does not use it. Chilies, both dried and fresh, are also used freely and both are included here. Tamarind provides the tang that balances the heat of the peppers and is a distinguishing feature of these seafood dishes. The dish should be spicy with the heat from the red chilies, but you can adjust that by controlling the number of pepper seeds you include. Serve with hot cooked rice or an Indian bread.

3 lbs	catfish, red snapper or similarly thick fish fillets	1.5 kg
3½ tbsp	vegetable oil, divided	52 mL
3 tbsp	coriander seeds	45 mL
2 tsp	urad dal (optional)	10 mL
1 tsp	black peppercorns	5 mL
½ tsp	fenugreek seeds (methi)	2 mL
15	dried red chilies, half with seeds removed	15
1 tsp	turmeric	5 mL
1 tsp	salt or to taste	5 mL
6 cups	finely chopped onions (6 to 8)	1.5 L
¾ cup	Thai tamarind purée, or 2 tbsp (25 mL) tamarind concentrate, diluted in ½ cup (125 mL) hot water	175 mL
30 to 40	fresh curry leaves (optional)	30 to 40
¼ cup	slivered peeled gingerroot	50 mL
6 to 8	green chilies, preferably serranos, slivered	6 to 8

1. Rinse fish and pat dry.

2. In a large heavy skillet, heat 1½ tbsp (22 mL) oil over medium heat. Sauté coriander seeds, dal, if using, peppercorns, fenugreek seeds and chilies, stirring continuously, until they turn slightly darker and aromatic, 3 to 4 minutes. Remove from skillet and grind to a powder in a spice grinder or coffee grinder that has been reserved only for spices. Add turmeric and salt. Mix well. Rub spice powder into fish and refrigerate, uncovered, for 1 hour.

3. In same skillet, heat remaining oil over medium–high heat. Sauté onions until light golden, about 10 minutes.

4. Stir in tamarind and ½ cup (125 mL) water. Arrange fish in single layer in skillet. Reduce heat to medium. Spoon gravy on top and cook, uncovered, until fish flakes when tested with a fork, 8 to 10 minutes. If gravy seems too dry, add ½ cup (125 mL) additional water while cooking. Sprinkle curry leaves, if using, ginger and green chilies on top. Cover and let stand for 5 minutes. Serve with rice or an Indian bread.

Goa Seafood Curry

Serves 8		

Goan food often uses quantities of dried red chilies. While Goan seafood curries are traditionally hot, I have removed some seeds to make it milder. Adjust the number of seeds included to suit your palate. Goa curry is always served with copious quantities of steamed rice.

TIP

Cachumber Salad:
In a bowl, combine 1 chopped ripe tomato, 1 chopped medium onion, 2 thinly sliced green chilies, preferably serranos, and juice of 1 lime or lemon. Refrigerator for at least 1 hour or for up to 6 hours.

MASALA PASTE

12	whole dried red chilies, half with seeds removed	12
2	green chilies, preferably serranos	2
15 to 18	cloves garlic	15 to 18
1	piece peeled gingerroot, 1 1/2 inches (4 cm) long	1
2 tsp	cumin seeds, freshly toasted	10 mL
2 tsp	poppy seeds	10 mL
1 tsp	turmeric	5 mL
1/4 cup	raw cashew nuts	50 mL
1/4 cup	white vinegar	50 mL
2 tbsp	vegetable oil	25 mL
4 cups	finely chopped onions (4 to 5)	1 L
1	can (14 oz/400 mL) coconut milk	1
2 1/2 tsp	salt or to taste	12 mL
2 lbs	medium shrimp, peeled and deveined	1 kg
1 lb	catfish, red snapper, halibut or any similar fish, skinned and cut into 3-by 2-inch (7.5 x 5 cm) pieces	500 g
4 to 5 tbsp	lime or lemon juice	60 to 75 mL
	Lemon wedges, for garnish	

1. *Masala Paste:* In a blender, combine red and green chilies, garlic, ginger, cumin and poppy seeds, turmeric, cashews, vinegar and 5 to 6 tbsp (75 to 90 mL) water. (Do not use a food processor.) Blend to a paste. Set aside.

2. In a deep skillet or large saucepan, heat oil over medium-high heat. Add onions and sauté until golden, 6 to 8 minutes.

3. Add spice paste and mix well. Reduce heat to medium-low and sauté, stirring frequently, 6 to 8 minutes. If necessary, deglaze pan with 1 tbsp (15 mL) water at a time to prevent sticking.

4. Stir in coconut milk and salt. Cover and bring to a boil. Simmer for about 5 minutes.

5. Increase heat and add shrimp and fish. Allow gravy to come to a boil again and reduce heat. Cover and cook until shrimp are opaque and fish flakes when tested with a fork, 8 to 10 minutes. Do not overcook. Stir in lime juice. Remove from heat and let stand, covered, for 15 minutes before serving to allow flavors to infuse seafood.

6. Serve hot with plain boiled rice, lemon wedges and Cachumber Salad (see Tip, left).

Amritsari Fish

This famous fried fish from Punjab uses local river fish. Carom seed, (ajwain) is the distinctive flavor here. Amritsar is an important city in Punjab, the seat of the Sikh religion, and this dish is a classic, perhaps the best known fish recipe in north Indian food. Punjab is land locked, so fish and seafood are not a feature of their diet. I am not sure how or why this dish got its name.

❋

TIP

Chaat masala is a blend of several spices, including ground dried pomegranate seeds and ground unripe dried green mango (amchur), which add sourness to the mix. It is used in the street foods of north India and the area around Mumbai. Packages of chaat masala are available in Indian stores.

◆ *Deep-fryer or wok*

4 lbs	fish steaks, such as halibut or any other firm fish (1/2 inch/2 cm thick)	2 kg
1/3 cup	cider vinegar	75 mL
4 tsp	salt or to taste, divided	20 mL
1 1/4 cups	chickpea flour (besan)	300 mL
3 tbsp	minced peeled gingerroot	45 mL
3 tbsp	minced garlic	45 mL
3 tbsp	carom seeds (ajwain)	45 mL
1 tsp	cayenne pepper	5 mL
1 tsp	freshly ground black pepper	5 mL
1/2 tsp	turmeric	2 mL
	Few drops orange food coloring (optional)	
	Vegetable oil for deep-frying	
2 to 3 tsp	chaat masala or 4 tsp (20 mL) freshly squeezed lemon juice (see Tip, left)	10 to 15 mL
	Lemon wedges, for garnish	

1. Rinse fish and pat dry. In a shallow dish, combine vinegar with 2 tsp (10 mL) of the salt. Add fish, turning to coat, and marinate in refrigerator for 30 minutes.

2. Meanwhile, mix chickpea flour with enough water (6 to 8 tbsp/90 to 125 mL) to make a thick smooth paste to coat and adhere to fish. Stir in ginger, garlic, carom seeds, cayenne pepper, black pepper, turmeric, remaining salt and food coloring, if using.

3. Drain fish and wipe dry. Coat fish with paste and set aside for 20 minutes.

4. Fill a deep-fryer or wok with 4 inches (10 cm) oil. Heat deep-fryer to 350°F (180°C) or place wok over medium heat. Add fish and deep-fry, in batches, until cooked through and crisp, 6 to 8 minutes per batch.

5. Sprinkle fish with chaat masala and serve with lemon wedges.

Preeti's Grilled Fish

My daughter-in-law Preeti, a superb cook, introduced me to this simple but fabulous dish several years ago. It continues to be one of my fallback recipes when I need to get dinner on the table in a hurry.

❋

TIP

Make a larger quantity of the garlic, cumin and chili mixture and store in the refrigerator, tightly covered, for up to 3 months. Use it to season chicken breasts or pork tenderloin before cooking. Stir in lemon juice just before using.

◆ *Preheat broiler*

3 lbs	catfish fillets or any other fish fillets	1.5 kg
8 to 10	cloves garlic	8 to 10
1 tbsp	cumin seeds	15 mL
8	dried red chilies, seeds removed	8
	Juice of 1 large lime or lemon	
2½ tsp	salt or to taste	12 mL
TOPPING		
1 tbsp	vegetable oil	15 mL
2 tbsp	chopped green chilies, preferably serranos	25 mL
1¼ cups	chopped tomatoes	300 mL
1 cup	sliced green onions, including some green part	250 mL
½ cup	cilantro, chopped	125 mL
	Lemon wedges or slices, for garnish	

1. Rinse fish and pat dry.

2. In a blender, grind together garlic, cumin seeds, red chilies and lime juice until a paste forms. Coat fish with paste and place on a baking sheet. Set aside for 15 minutes.

3. Grill fish in preheated broiler until it flakes easily with a fork, 6 to 8 minutes, depending on thickness of fillet. Sprinkle with salt.

4. *Topping:* Meanwhile, in a skillet, heat oil over medium heat. Sauté chilies for 1 minute. Add tomatoes and green onions. Sauté for 2 minutes. Stir in cilantro and remove from heat.

5. Arrange fish on serving platter. Top with vegetables. Garnish with lemon wedges.

Baked Fish Fillets
with Yogurt Topping

An easy but impressive dish, this recipe has a topping that keeps the fish moist while imparting outstanding flavor.

TIP

The yogurt topping can be made up to 2 days ahead and refrigerated.

◆ *Preheat oven to 400°F (200°C)*
◆ *Baking sheet, lined with foil*

2 to	catfish fillets, or any other similarly	1 to
2½ lbs	thick fillet, such as cod or red snapper	1.25 kg
½ tsp	turmeric	2 mL
2½ tsp	salt or to taste	12 mL
5 tbsp	vegetable oil, divided	75 mL
3 cups	chopped red onions (about 2 large)	750 mL
3 cups	plain yogurt, well drained	750 mL
2 tsp	coriander powder	10 mL
1 tsp	cayenne pepper	5 mL
½ tsp	garam masala	2 mL
1 cup	cilantro, coarsely chopped	250 mL
2 tsp	minced peeled gingerroot	10 mL
2 tsp	minced garlic	10 mL
1 cup	chopped Roma tomato	250 mL
3 to	lemon juice	45 to
4 tbsp		60 mL
	Cucumber slices, for garnish	

1. Rinse fish and pat dry. Rub turmeric and 1½ tsp (7 mL) salt into fish and set aside for 15 minutes. (Can be refrigerated for several hours.)

2. In a skillet, heat 2 tbsp (25 mL) oil over medium-high heat. Sauté onions until softened and no moisture is left, 6 to 8 minutes. Let cool. Stir onions and any oil remaining in pan into yogurt. Add coriander, cayenne pepper, garam masala, cilantro, ginger, garlic and tomato. Stir in lemon juice and remaining salt. Mix well.

3. In same skillet, heat remaining oil. Partially fry fish on each side, but do not cook through. Transfer to prepared baking sheet. Spread yogurt mixture over fish. Bake in preheated oven for 30 minutes if fillets are large, or 20 to 25 minutes if smaller. Test center of fillets with fork to see if fish flakes easily and cook longer, if necessary.

4. Transfer to a serving platter and garnish with cucumber slices.

Bengali Mustard Fish

2 lbs	fish fillets, such as red snapper, catfish or any other similar fish	1 kg
1 1/4 tsp	turmeric	6 mL
1 1/2 tsp	salt or to taste	7 mL
6 cups	coarsely chopped onions (about 3 large)	1.5 L
8	green chilies, preferably serranos, divided (see Tips, left)	8
1 tbsp	Indian mustard powder or any good-quality mustard powder	15 mL
1 tsp	cayenne pepper	5 mL
1/4 cup	mustard oil (see Tips, left)	50 mL
2 tsp	nigella seeds (kalaunji)	10 mL
	Hot cooked rice	

Serves 8

This is a classic dish from Bengal, where mustard is the most popular spice. It is used extensively in the form of dark mustard seeds, mustard powder and also mustard oil.

TIPS

Green chilies are not too hot when cooked, but use fewer if you want a milder dish, rather than scrape out seeds.

Mustard oil is cold-pressed from dark mustard seeds and has a very strong aroma and flavor. It is available in Indian markets.

1. Rinse fish and pat dry.

2. Combine turmeric, salt and a little water to make a paste. Coat fish on both sides with paste and set aside for 15 minutes.

3. Meanwhile, in a food processor, combine onions, 2 chilies, mustard powder and cayenne pepper to make a paste.

4. In a large skillet, heat mustard oil over high heat until smoking, 2 to 3 minutes. Turn off heat and let cool for 1 minute. Remove 1 tbsp (15 mL) of the oil and set aside. Reheat skillet to medium heat. Partially fry fish to seal. Transfer with slotted spoon to a dish.

5. In same skillet over medium heat, add nigella seeds and sauté until fragrant, about 1 minute. Add onion paste and sauté for 5 to 6 minutes. Pour in 3/4 cup (175 mL) water. Mix well and bring to a gentle boil.

6. Return fish to skillet. Cut remaining green chilies in half lengthwise and scatter over top. Drizzle reserved oil on top of fish. Cover and cook over medium-low heat until fish flakes easily with a fork, 6 to 8 minutes. Serve with steamed rice.

Stuffed Fish with Garlic Herb Topping

I urge you to get the freshest fish possible for this heavenly dish. Sweet caramelized onions balanced with a healthy dose of cayenne make a stuffing that is the essence of simplicity yet complex in its flavors.

* *Preheat oven to 375°F (190°C)*
* *Baking sheet, lined with foil*

3 to 3½ lbs	whole fish, such as red snapper, red fish or other similar fish	1.5 to 1.75 kg
1	lime or lemon	1
2½ tsp	salt or to taste	12 mL

STUFFING

1½ tbsp	vegetable oil	22 mL
4 cups	finely sliced onions (about 4)	1 L
1 tbsp	minced peeled gingerroot	15 mL
2 tsp	minced garlic	10 mL
1 tsp	cayenne pepper	5 mL
¾ tsp	salt or to taste	4 mL
1 cup	mint leaves, chopped	250 mL
1 cup	cilantro leaves, chopped	250 mL

TOPPING

1 tbsp	vegetable oil	15 mL
⅓ cup	coarsely chopped garlic (about 1 large head)	75 mL
¾ cup	sliced green onions (3 to 4)	175 mL
2 cups	mint leaves, loosely packed	500 mL
2 cups	cilantro, loosely packed	500 mL

1. Scale and clean fish, removing center bone. Do not remove head and tail. Score skin on both sides of fish. Rub all over with lime and salt. Cover and refrigerate for at least 1 hour or up to 2 hours.

2. *Stuffing:* In a skillet, heat oil over medium–high heat. Sauté onions, stirring occasionally, until deep brown, 15 to 20 minutes. Stir in ginger, garlic, cayenne and salt. Cook for 2 minutes. Remove from heat. Stir in mint and cilantro.

3. Place fish on prepared baking sheet. Stuff with mixture. Bake in preheated oven for 30 minutes or until fish flakes easily with a fork. Peel off skin from top of fish. Transfer to serving platter and keep warm.

4. *Topping:* In a small saucepan, heat oil over medium heat. Sauté garlic until golden and fragrant, about 2 minutes. Stir in green onions and cook for 2 minutes. Add mint and cilantro and cook for 2 minutes longer. Spoon over fish and serve immediately.

Coconut Chutney–Coated Fish Parcels

A classic dish of the Parsis of Mumbai (Bombay), this is a showstopping entrée. I like to serve it with a spicy dal and steamed rice.

TIPS

Coconut chutney can be made 2 days ahead and refrigerated, tightly covered. Chutney can also be frozen for up to 3 months.

♦

If banana leaves are unavailable, use foil to wrap fish. Leave foil slightly loose to allow steam to circulate.

♦ *Steamer*

8	banana leaf sections, each about 12 inches (30 cm) long (see Tips, left)	8
	Vegetable spray	
3 cups	grated fresh or frozen coconut (thawed if frozen)	750 mL
12	cloves garlic	12
4	green chilies, preferably serranos (2 inches/5 cm long)	4
2 tsp	cumin seeds	10 mL
1 tsp	granulated sugar	5 mL
1 tsp	salt or to taste	5 mL
	Juice of 1 lime or lemon	
4 cups	cilantro leaves, including soft stems	1 L
8	halibut steaks or any similar fish (1 inch/2.5 cm thick)	8
¼ cup	white vinegar	50 mL

1. Rinse and wipe banana leaves and trim any dry ends. Lay one leaf on work surface, rib side up. Using a sharp knife held almost horizontally (knife should be almost parallel to work surface), carefully slice away part of thick rib, if necessary. Spray dull side with vegetable spray. Repeat with remaining leaves.

2. In a food processor, process coconut, garlic, chilies, cumin seeds, sugar and salt until coarse. Add lime juice, then cilantro, in batches, processing until fine and scraping sides of bowl frequently. Transfer to a bowl.

3. Carefully coat each piece of fish on both sides with ¼-inch (0.5 cm) thick paste. Place one piece of coated fish 3 inches (7.5 cm) from end of oiled side of banana leaf. Cover with 3-inch (7.5 cm) flap. Fold in sides and continue to fold into a "parcel." Secure with kitchen twine. Repeat with remaining fish and leaves.

4. Fill steamer with 1½ inches (4 cm) water. Add vinegar. Place wrapped fish in steamer and cook for about 30 minutes. To serve, place parcels on platter and allow each person to unwrap package.

Mohini's Spicy Shrimp

Serves 8

My mother's cousin, Mohini, had a wonderful cook who did an especially fine job with this dish. The dried mango powder used for its tartness adds an interesting note.

TIP

You can make this recipe ahead up to Step 4. Reheat masala until it is cooking rapidly and stir in shrimp just before you plan to serve.

♦ *Large wok or saucepan*

2 lbs	shrimp, peeled and deveined	1 kg
2 tsp	cayenne pepper, divided	2 mL
1 tsp	turmeric, divided	5 mL
1 1/2 tsp	salt or to taste	7 mL
	Juice of 1 lemon or lime	
1 tbsp	minced peeled gingerroot	15 mL
1 tbsp	minced garlic	15 mL
2 tsp	coriander powder	10 mL
2 tsp	cumin powder	10 mL
2 tsp	mango powder (amchur) or 3 tbsp (45 mL) freshly squeezed lemon juice	10 mL
2 tbsp	vegetable oil	25 mL
1	can (7 1/2 oz/213 g) tomato sauce	1
1/3 cup	cilantro, chopped	75 mL

1. Mix shrimp with 1/2 tsp (2 mL) of the cayenne pepper, 1/4 tsp (1 mL) of the turmeric, salt and lemon juice. Set aside.

2. Meanwhile, in a blender, combine ginger, garlic, coriander, cumin and mango powders, remaining cayenne pepper and 3 tbsp (45 mL) water to make a paste.

3. In a large wok or saucepan, heat oil over medium heat. Sauté masala paste and remaining turmeric until masala is fragrant, 4 to 5 minutes.

4. Stir in tomato sauce and cook until reduced by about one-third.

5. Increase heat to high and mix in shrimp. Cook until shrimp turn opaque, 4 to 5 minutes. Do not overcook.

6. Fold in cilantro and serve immediately.

Spicy Sweet-and-Sour Shrimp

I love to serve these shrimp over pasta, even though that is not entirely Indian. The assertive flavors are perfect with the blandness and texture of the pasta. Sometimes, I sauté a cup of sliced bell peppers, a vegetable popular in India, with the tomatoes.

❋

◆ *Large wok*

2 tbsp	vegetable oil	25 mL
1 cup	finely chopped onion (about 1 large)	250 mL
1 1/2 tbsp	minced garlic	22 mL
1 tbsp	minced peeled gingerroot	15 mL
2	large tomatoes, cut into 1-inch (2.5 cm) wedges	2
1 1/2 tsp	salt or to taste	7 mL
1 tsp	turmeric	5 mL
1 tsp	cayenne pepper	5 mL
1 tsp	coriander powder	5 mL
2 tsp	granulated sugar	10 mL
1/3 cup	white vinegar	75 mL
2 lbs	shrimp, peeled and deveined	1 kg
3 tbsp	cilantro, chopped	45 mL

1. In a wok or heavy skillet, heat oil over medium–high heat. Sauté onion until golden, about 5 minutes. Add garlic and ginger and sauté for 5 minutes.

2. Add tomatoes and salt. Cook for 5 minutes, then mash slightly with the back of a spoon. Add turmeric, cayenne and coriander. Mix well and sauté for 3 to 4 minutes.

3. Stir in sugar and vinegar. Increase heat to high and bring to a boil. Add shrimp and cook until shrimp turn opaque, 4 to 5 minutes. Do not overcook. There should be a thick masala coating the shrimp.

4. Garnish with chopped cilantro to serve.

Prawn Patia

Serves 8		

This classic dish of the Parsi community was my favorite at Parsi weddings. It's hot and spicy and not for the faint of heart. To make it milder, remove some of the red chili seeds.

❋

MASALA

10 to 14	dried red chilies, half with seeds removed	10 to 14
20	large cloves garlic	20
1	piece peeled gingerroot, 1 inch (2.5 cm) long	1
2 tbsp	poppy seeds	25 mL
2 tsp	coriander powder	10 mL
2 tsp	cumin powder	10 mL
¾ tsp	turmeric	4 mL
½ tsp	black peppercorns	2 mL
¼ cup	red wine vinegar	50 mL
2 tbsp	vegetable oil	25 mL
3 cups	finely chopped onions (3 to 4)	750 mL
5 cups	chopped tomatoes (6 to 7)	1.25 L
1½ tsp	salt or to taste	7 mL
1 tsp	granulated sugar	5 mL
2 lbs	shrimp, peeled and deveined	1 kg
2 cups	cilantro, chopped, divided	500 mL

1. *Masala:* Soak red chilies in hot water for 15 minutes. Drain and place in a blender with garlic, ginger, poppy seeds, coriander, cumin, turmeric, peppercorns and vinegar. Blend to as fine a paste as possible. Set aside.

2. In a large saucepan, heat oil over medium-high heat. Sauté onions until golden brown, 8 to 10 minutes.

3. Stir in masala paste and sauté, stirring often to prevent burning, until dark, 2 to 3 minutes.

4. Reduce heat to medium-low. Add tomatoes and salt. Cover and cook until very soft, 5 to 6 minutes. Mash with back of spoon. Add sugar and cook, stirring continuously, for 2 to 3 minutes.

5. Increase heat to medium-high. Add shrimp and 1 cup (250 mL) of the cilantro. Mix well, and cook, uncovered, until shrimp are opaque, 4 to 5 minutes. Do not overcook.

6. Stir in remaining cilantro just before serving.

Golden Shrimp with Cilantro and Lime

Anthony, the cook at our beach house outside Mumbai, would often go down to the ocean to meet the fishing boats as they came in. He invented this simple dish using just-caught shrimp, and it quickly became popular with friends and family.

TIP

Serve over a bed of greens as a first course or as an entrée. I also like to serve it as a cocktail appetizer or as part of a buffet.

8	cloves garlic	8
2 tsp	salt	10 mL
3 lbs	shrimp, peeled and deveined	1.5 kg
1	bay leaf	1
1/2 cup	lime juice, divided	125 mL
2 1/4 tsp	turmeric, divided	11 mL
1 tsp	cayenne pepper	5 mL
1/2 cup	cilantro leaves, divided	125 mL

1. Mash garlic and salt to a paste with a mortar and pestle and rub into shrimp. Set aside for 15 minutes.

2. In a large saucepan over medium–high heat, combine 8 cups (2 L) water, bay leaf, 1 tbsp (15 mL) of the lime juice and 2 tsp (10 mL) of the turmeric. Bring to a boil. When water is boiling, stir in shrimp and cook just until opaque, 2 to 3 minutes. Do not overcook. Drain and transfer shrimp to a bowl.

3. Stir together remaining turmeric, cayenne pepper and remaining lime juice. Pour over warm shrimp. Toss until well combined.

4. Chop half of the cilantro leaves and add to cooled shrimp. Add remaining whole leaves and toss. Adjust seasonings and refrigerate for at least 3 hours before serving.

Cilantro Pickled Shrimp

Makes about 1½ cups (375 mL)

This unusual recipe can be enjoyed both as an appetizer and a condiment. The key is to serve small portions since it is highly seasoned. Serve as an accompaniment to dal and rice or as a condiment with an Indian bread, such as a stuffed paratha, along with a raita.

TIP

Pickled shrimp keeps well in a jar for up to 2 weeks in the refrigerator. Heat ½ cup (125 mL) additional oil in a pan to smoking point on medium-high heat, 3 to 4 minutes. Let cool and pour in jar to completely cover shrimp. Cover jar and refrigerate.

◆ *Small wok or saucepan*

8 oz	small shrimp, peeled and deveined	250 g
⅔ cup	vegetable oil, divided	150 mL
¾ tsp	asafetida (hing)	4 mL
2 tsp	cayenne pepper	10 mL
1 tsp	coriander powder	5 mL
½ tsp	turmeric	2 mL
½ tsp	fenugreek powder	2 mL
½ tsp	crushed mustard seeds	2 mL
1½ tsp	salt or to taste	7 mL
6 tbsp	lemon juice, divided	90 mL
2½ tbsp	minced garlic	32 mL
1 tsp	poppy seeds	5 mL
4	green chilies, preferably serranos, minced	4
4 cups	cilantro, with soft stems, chopped coarsely	1 L

1. Rinse shrimp and pat dry.

2. In a small wok or saucepan, heat 2 tbsp (25 mL) of the oil over medium-high heat until very hot. Add asafetida and when it stops sizzling in about 20 seconds, add shrimp and sauté until they turn opaque, about 2 minutes.

3. Add cayenne pepper, coriander, turmeric, fenugreek, mustard seeds and salt. Sauté for 3 to 4 minutes, adjusting heat to prevent burning masala. Stir in 2 tbsp (25 mL) of the lemon juice and remove from heat.

4. In another saucepan, heat remaining oil over medium heat. Add garlic and sauté for 1 minute. Add poppy seeds and chilies. Sauté for 1 minute. Add cilantro and stir-fry for 2 minutes.

5. Pour cilantro mixture over shrimp and return to medium heat. Add remaining lemon juice and mix well. When lemon juice is absorbed, remove from heat.

Mussels in Cilantro Broth

<table>
<tr><td>2 lbs</td><td>mussels, scrubbed</td><td>1 kg</td></tr>
<tr><td>4 cups</td><td>cilantro, with stems</td><td>1 L</td></tr>
<tr><td>1</td><td>head garlic, about 20 cloves</td><td>1</td></tr>
<tr><td>6 to 8</td><td>green chilies, preferably serranos</td><td>6 to 8</td></tr>
<tr><td>6 tbsp</td><td>grated fresh or frozen coconut (thawed if frozen)</td><td>90 mL</td></tr>
<tr><td>2 tbsp</td><td>vegetable oil</td><td>25 mL</td></tr>
<tr><td>1 tsp</td><td>cumin seeds</td><td>5 mL</td></tr>
<tr><td>4 cups</td><td>finely chopped onions (4 to 5)</td><td>1 L</td></tr>
<tr><td>2½ tsp</td><td>salt or to taste</td><td>12 mL</td></tr>
</table>

Serves 8

The original recipe for this heavenly dish uses tesri (littleneck clams), which are plentiful on the west coast of India. Mussels are easier to find than clams and are a very good substitute.

TIP

Traditionally, this dish is not served as a soup but rather as part of the meal, with chapati. I like to serve it as a soup or entrée with lots of French bread and a salad.

1. In a large saucepan over medium–high heat, combine mussels and 8 cups (2 L) water. Cover and bring to a boil. Reduce heat to medium–low and simmer for 2 to 3 minutes or until mussels open. Do not overcook. Discard any that remain closed. Drain, reserving liquid. Strain liquid through a coffee filter and set aside.

2. In a blender, combine cilantro, garlic, chilies, coconut and 4 to 5 tbsp (60 to 75 mL) water. Blend to a fine paste. Set aside.

3. In a large saucepan, heat oil over medium heat. Add cumin seeds and sauté until fragrant, about 1 minute. Add onions and sauté until soft but not brown, about 10 minutes.

4. Pour reserved liquid and 4 cups (1 L) water into pan. Stir in salt. Increase heat to medium–high and bring to a boil. Reduce heat to medium–low and simmer, covered, for 5 minutes. Add mussels and simmer, uncovered, for 3 to 4 minutes.

5. Stir in cilantro paste and heat through. Serve immediately.

Vegetarian Entrées

INDIAN FOOD, LIKE many other Eastern cuisines, often uses meat and poultry as an ingredient rather than making it the focus of a meal. My father, who enjoyed meat more than anyone else in the family, always said one meal with an animal protein was all that the body could handle, so the other meal would generally be vegetarian. Fortunately, Indian food excels in vegetarian dishes, with an astonishing variety in flavors and textures. Hearty vegetable stews, tasty ragouts of beans and vegetables, spinach combined with an assortment of vegetables — these and many more delicious dishes make for some wonderful food memories. In addition to the amazing variety of vegetables available in India, variations in regional cooking styles have added to the infinite possibilities. Is it any wonder, then, that Indians are so in love with vegetables?

Many Indians are vegetarian for religious reasons. Their protein comes from beans and lentils (see Beans and Lentils chapter). Often, these are cooked with vegetables and make wonderfully satisfying vegetarian entrées. Fresh and dried peas, such as black-eyed peas, also combine well with vegetables, resulting in mouth-watering main dishes. Stuffed vegetables are also popular and make impressive entrées.

Eggs, although not considered strictly vegetarian, are acceptable to some vegetarians. The Indian diet uses eggs rather sparingly, and even desserts generally tend to be egg-free. Included in this chapter are a few egg dishes that have become part of the food vocabulary, particularly in cities like Mumbai, where they are an affordable breakfast or lunch to go.

Many of these dishes can be refrigerated for several days, and some are suitable for freezing. So make enough to last beyond one meal and the time spent will be well rewarded.

❄ ❄ ❄

Akoori
Indian Scrambled Eggs

Serves 4 to 6

Weekend breakfasts in our home often meant a big dish of Akoori, spiced scrambled eggs with onions and tomatoes, piled high on buttered toast. The dish is of Parsi origin and much loved by Mumbaiites.

❋

TIP

Akoori is wonderful as a filling for a wrap or stuffed into pita bread.

8	eggs	8
1 tsp	salt or to taste	5 mL
1/4 tsp	freshly ground black pepper	1 mL
3 tbsp	vegetable oil	45 mL
1 tsp	cumin seeds	5 mL
1 cup	chopped onion	250 mL
2 tsp	finely chopped green chilies, preferably serranos	10 mL
1 cup	chopped tomato	250 mL
1/2 tsp	cayenne pepper	2 mL
1/4 tsp	turmeric	1 mL
1/4 cup	cilantro, chopped	50 mL
	Tomato wedges and cilantro sprigs, for garnish	

1. In a bowl, gently whisk eggs, salt and pepper. Do not beat.

2. In a large skillet, heat oil over medium–high heat and add cumin seeds. Stir in onion and green chilies and sauté until golden, 3 to 4 minutes.

3. Add tomato and sauté, stirring continuously, for 1 minute. Stir in cayenne, turmeric and cilantro. Cook for 1 minute longer. Reduce heat to medium–low and slowly add egg mixture. Cook, stirring gently, until eggs are soft and creamy, 3 to 4 minutes. Do not overcook.

4. Serve garnished with tomato wedges and cilantro sprigs.

Aamlete

Indian Omelet

Serves 4		

Aamlete is very popular with urban Indians. Served in every corner tea shop in Mumbai for breakfast or lunch, it is also offered on breakfast menus on Indian trains. Aamlete sandwiches served with ketchup (called tomato sauce) are standard lunch fare on the streets of Mumbai, when office workers are looking for fast food.

❋

TIP

Aamletes are traditionally flatter and not as fluffy as an omelet, and are often served with hot buttered toast or sandwiched between 2 slices of thin sandwich bread.

6	eggs	6
1 tsp	salt	5 mL
¼ tsp	freshly ground black pepper	1 mL
2 to 3 tbsp	vegetable oil, divided	25 to 45 mL
¾ cup	chopped onion, divided	175 mL
¾ cup	chopped tomato, divided	175 mL
2 tsp	chopped green chilies, preferably serranos, divided	10 mL
¼ cup	cilantro, chopped, divided	50 mL

1. In a bowl, beat together eggs, salt, pepper and 2 tbsp (25 mL) water until blended.

2. In a large nonstick skillet, heat 1 tbsp (15 mL) of the oil over medium heat. Pour one-quarter of the eggs into skillet. Scatter one-quarter each of the onion, tomato, chilies and cilantro evenly on top. Cook, without stirring, until edges can be lifted with spatula, about 2 minutes. Fold over to form semicircle. Cook for 30 seconds longer.

3. Transfer to platter and keep warm. Repeat to make remaining 3 omelets, adding enough oil between batches to prevent sticking.

Egg Curry

*There are many
variations on Egg Curry,
depending on the region.
In my family, this simple,
light version wins the
most votes.*

TIP

Egg curry is delicious
with rice, an Indian
bread, or soft dinner
rolls split in half and
topped with the curry.
Make sure the gravy
completely soaks the roll.
Sprinkle with additional
chopped cilantro.

2 tbsp	vegetable oil	25 mL
2 cups	finely chopped onions (2 to 3)	500 mL
1 tbsp	minced peeled gingerroot	15 mL
1 tbsp	minced garlic	15 mL
1 tbsp	minced green chilies	15 mL
1 1/2 tbsp	coriander powder	22 mL
3/4 tsp	turmeric	4 mL
1/2 tsp	cayenne pepper	2 mL
1/2 tsp	cumin powder	2 mL
1	can (28 oz/796 mL) tomatoes, puréed with liquid	1
1 1/2 tsp	salt or to taste	7 mL
12	hard-cooked eggs, peeled and halved	12
1/2 tsp	garam masala	2 mL
	Juice of 1 lime or lemon	
1/4 cup	cilantro, chopped	50 mL

1. In a large saucepan, heat oil over medium-high heat.
   Sauté onions until beginning to color, 4 to 6 minutes.
   Reduce heat to medium and sauté until browned,
   8 to 10 minutes. Stir in ginger, garlic and chilies and
   cook for 2 minutes.

2. Stir in coriander, turmeric, cayenne pepper and cumin.
   Cook for 2 to 3 minutes, stirring continuously.

3. Pour in tomatoes and salt. Mix well. Reduce heat to
   low, cover and simmer, stirring occasionally, until
   gravy is thickened, 8 to 10 minutes.

4. Place halved eggs in single layer in pan. Spoon gravy
   on top of eggs and simmer, uncovered, for 5 minutes
   longer.

5. Remove from heat. Sprinkle with garam masala and
   lime juice. Cover and let stand for 5 minutes.

6. Garnish with cilantro to serve.

Indian Scrambled Eggs *(Akoori)* (page 126)

Left to right: Hot Pineapple Chutney (page 169),
Tomato Raita (page 162), Sweet Mango Chutney
(page 170) and Cabbage and Apple Raita (page 164)

Saag Panir
Curried Spinach and Cheese

This recipe is an amazingly successful light version of a very popular north Indian classic. This creamy dish seems sinfully rich but is instead guilt-free.

TIP

The spinach mixture should be creamy. If too dry, add a little more yogurt. This dish freezes well. Reheat in microwave on Medium, or on the stove over low heat.

2 tbsp	vegetable oil	25 mL
1 1/2 cups	chopped onion	375 mL
1 tbsp	minced peeled gingerroot	15 mL
3	minced green chilies, preferably serranos	3
2 tsp	coriander powder	10 mL
1 tsp	turmeric	5 mL
2	packages (each 10 oz/300 g) frozen spinach, thawed	2
1 1/2 tsp	salt or to taste	7 mL
1 cup	nonfat milk	250 mL
2 cups	plain nonfat yogurt, at room temperature	500 mL
2 tsp	cornstarch	10 mL
1	batch Lower-Fat Panir, cut into 1/2-inch (1 cm) cubes (see recipe, page 140)	1

1. In a large saucepan, heat oil over medium–high heat. Sauté onion, ginger and chilies until softened and pale golden, 5 to 8 minutes.

2. Reduce heat to medium and stir in coriander and turmeric. Sauté, stirring well, for 2 to 3 minutes.

3. Mix in spinach and salt. Cover and simmer for 5 minutes. Remove from heat.

4. In a blender, purée spinach mixture with milk.

5. Reduce heat to low and return mixture to stove. Stir together yogurt and cornstarch to creamy consistency. Stir into spinach mixture. Add panir and mix thoroughly but gently. Cover and simmer for 10 to 12 minutes to heat through. Serve with Indian bread.

Hena's Finger Potatoes (page 145)

Sai Bhaji
Sindhi Spinach

Serves 10 to 12

This is the most popular vegetable dish in Sindhi cuisine. A light and nutritious combination of greens, vegetables and split yellow peas, it is served daily in most Sindhi homes in the summer, along with rice and plain yogurt. I love to eat it with a slice of white bread, which is also quite traditional.

TIPS

Sindhi Spinach freezes well in an airtight container for up to 6 months.

◆

If it appears too thick and dry after reheating, stir in 2 to 3 tbsp (25 to 45 mL) water to loosen it.

1 cup	split yellow peas (channa dal)	250 mL
1 tbsp	vegetable oil	15 mL
1½ tsp	cumin seeds	7 mL
2 tbsp	chopped green chilies, preferably serranos	25 mL
1 tbsp	minced peeled gingerroot	15 mL
1 tbsp	chopped garlic	15 mL
1	medium onion, chopped	1
1	red or green bell pepper, chopped	1
1	piece eggplant (3 inches/7.5 cm), cut into 1-inch (2.5 cm) dice	1
15	green beans, cut into ½-inch (1 cm) pieces	15
1	carrot, cut into ½-inch (1 cm) pieces	1
1	medium potato, cut into 1-inch (2.5 cm) dice	1
2	Roma tomatoes, chopped	2
1 tsp	turmeric	5 mL
2	packages (each 10 oz/300 g) frozen spinach, preferably thawed	2
½ cup	fresh dill, chopped, or 2 tbsp (25 mL) dried dill	125 mL
2½ tsp	salt or to taste	12 mL
¼ cup	Thai tamarind paste or 2 tbsp (25 mL) Indian tamarind concentrate	50 mL

1. Clean and pick through peas for any small stones and grit. Rinse several times in cold water until water is fairly clear. Soak in 3 cups (750 mL) water in a bowl for 30 minutes. Drain.

2. In a large saucepan, heat oil over medium heat. Add cumin seeds and sauté for 30 seconds. Add chilies, ginger and garlic. Sauté for 1 minute. Add onion, bell pepper, eggplant, beans, carrot, potato, tomatoes and turmeric. Mix well.

3. Add spinach, dill and drained peas. Pour in $1\frac{1}{2}$ cups (375 mL) water. Mix well. Increase heat to medium–high. Cover and bring to a boil. Reduce heat to medium and cook until peas and vegetables are softened, about 30 minutes.

4. Stir in salt and tamarind. Mash with potato masher or with back of spoon so vegetables and peas are well mixed. Continue to cook, uncovered, until mixture is thick, 10 to 15 minutes. Vegetables should be almost completely mashed and about half of the peas should also be mashed. Consistency will be thick but not dry. Serve with rice.

Creamy Spinach with Mung Dal

The creamy dal gives this lightly spiced spinach dish a sensually silky texture.

❋

1 cup	yellow mung beans (yellow mung dal)	250 mL
3 cups	chopped fresh spinach	750 mL
2 tbsp	minced green chilies, preferably serranos	25 mL
1 1/2 tbsp	minced peeled gingerroot	22 mL
1/2 tsp	turmeric	2 mL
2 tbsp	vegetable oil	25 mL
1 cup	finely chopped onion	250 mL
1/2 tsp	cayenne pepper	2 mL
1 1/2 tsp	salt or to taste	7 mL
1/4 cup	plain nonfat yogurt, divided	50 mL

1. Clean and pick through beans for any small stones and grit. Rinse several times in cold water until water is fairly clear. Soak in 3 cups (750 mL) water in a large saucepan for 10 minutes.

2. Add spinach, green chilies, ginger and turmeric to beans. Bring to a boil over medium heat, partially covered. Reduce heat to medium-low and simmer until dal is very soft, about 30 minutes. Remove from heat and purée with an immersion blender or in a blender.

3. In a medium saucepan, heat oil over medium-high heat. Sauté onion until golden, 6 to 8 minutes.

4. Stir in cayenne pepper and salt and sauté for 1 minute. Pour in dal mixture and mix well.

5. Stir yogurt until creamy. Add 2 tbsp (25 mL) of the yogurt to dal and mix. If too thick, add 1/2 cup (125 mL) hot water. Cover and simmer for 5 minutes.

6. Serve hot. Swirl remaining yogurt on top.

Potatoes in Tomato Gravy

Indians consider the potato to be a vegetable, so serving potato curry with rice is perfectly logical. Alternatively, serve with an Indian bread to scoop up the gravy.

VARIATION

Add 1½ cups (375 mL) peas for a variation. Small boiling onions, 1½ to 2 cups (375 to 500 mL), are also a good addition.

1 tbsp	vegetable oil	15 mL
1½ tsp	cumin seeds	7 mL
1½ tbsp	finely sliced green chilies, preferably serranos	22 mL
1	can (28 oz/796 mL) tomatoes, chopped or processed, including liquid	1
¾ tsp	turmeric	4 mL
2 lbs	all-purpose potatoes, peeled, cut into 1-inch (2.5 cm) cubes	1 kg
2 tsp	salt or to taste	10 mL
5 tbsp	cilantro, chopped, divided	75 mL

1. In a saucepan, heat oil over medium–high heat. Add cumin seeds and green chilies. Sauté until cumin is fragrant and slightly darker, about 1 minute.

2. Add tomatoes with juice and turmeric. Mix well. Bring to a boil. Cook for 2 minutes.

3. Add potatoes, salt and ¼ cup (50 mL) of the cilantro. Return to a boil. Reduce heat to low. Cover and simmer until potatoes are soft, 12 to 15 minutes. If gravy is too thin, mash a few potatoes with back of spoon and cook for 3 to 4 minutes longer to thicken.

4. Garnish with remaining cilantro to serve.

Corn and Vegetable Curry

Serves 8

A substantial main dish for vegetarians, this curry is particularly good in the summer, when corn and tomatoes are at their best.

TIP

If you are pressed for time, use frozen mixed vegetables straight from the bag, without thawing.

1 1/2 cups	diced potatoes (1/2-inch/1 cm dice)	375 mL
1 cup	diced green beans (1/2-inch/1 cm pieces)	250 mL
1/2 cup	diced carrots	125 mL
2 tbsp	vegetable oil	25 mL
3/4 tsp	mustard seeds	4 mL
10 to 12	fresh curry leaves (optional)	10 to 12
2 cups	corn kernels, fresh or frozen, thawed	500 mL
3 cups	chopped tomatoes	750 mL
1/2 cup	frozen peas, thawed	125 mL
4 oz	mushrooms, sliced	125 g
1 tbsp	minced peeled gingerroot	15 mL
2 1/2 tbsp	minced green chilies, preferably serranos	32 mL
1/2 tsp	granulated sugar	2 mL
1 1/2 tsp	salt or to taste	7 mL
1/4 cup	grated fresh coconut	50 mL
1 cup	cilantro, chopped, divided	250 mL

1. In a saucepan over medium–high heat, bring 4 cups (1 L) water to a boil. Add potatoes, beans and carrots. Return to a boil and reduce heat to medium. Cover and cook for 3 minutes. Drain and set aside.

2. In a large saucepan or wok, heat oil over high heat until a couple of mustard seeds thrown in start to sputter. Add remaining mustard seeds and cover quickly. When seeds stop popping, in a few seconds, uncover, reduce heat to medium and add curry leaves, if using. Sauté for 1 minute.

3. Add reserved vegetables, corn, tomatoes, peas, mushrooms, ginger, chilies, sugar and salt. Mix well. Cover and cook until vegetables are tender, about 5 minutes. Add coconut and 1/2 cup (125 mL) of the cilantro. Toss and cook for 1 minute.

4. Garnish with remaining cilantro and serve with rice or an Indian bread.

Black-Eyed Peas with Vegetables

This hearty stew is a perfect vegetarian entrée. It is a recipe from a friend in Austin, Texas, who is a wizard with vegetarian dishes.

1½ tbsp	vegetable oil	22 mL
1 tsp	mustard seeds	5 mL
½ tsp	cumin seeds	2 mL
¼ tsp	fenugreek seeds (methi)	1 mL
1 cup	finely chopped onion	250 mL
2½ tsp	sambar powder	12 mL
1 tsp	garam masala	5 mL
2 to 3	green chilies, preferably serranos	2 to 3
1	package (11 oz/330 g) fresh or frozen black-eyed peas	1
1 tsp	minced peeled gingerroot	5 mL
1 tsp	minced garlic	5 mL
1½ tsp	salt or to taste	7 mL
½ cup	cubed potatoes (1-inch/2.5 cm cubes)	125 mL
½ cup	sliced carrots (½ inch/1 cm thick)	125 mL
½ cup	chopped green beans (½-inch/1 cm pieces)	125 mL

1. In a medium saucepan, heat oil over high heat until a couple of mustard seeds thrown in start to sputter. Add remaining mustard seeds and cover quickly.

2. When the seeds stop popping, in a few seconds, uncover, reduce heat to medium and add cumin and fenugreek seeds. Sauté for 10 seconds. Add onion and sauté until golden, 5 to 7 minutes.

3. Add sambar powder, garam masala and green chilies. Mix well. Cook for 2 minutes. Add black eyed-peas, ginger and garlic. Mix well. Add 3 cups (750 mL) water. Cover and bring to a boil. Reduce heat to low. Simmer until peas are slightly softened, about 20 minutes. Stir in salt.

4. Add potatoes, carrots and beans and cook until vegetables are tender, 12 to 15 minutes. If necessary, add ½ cup (125 mL) hot water to allow for a thick gravy.

5. Serve with rice or an Indian bread.

Whole Baked Masala Cauliflower

This elegant dish from north India is particularly wonderful in the cooler months, when cauliflower is at its best.

TIP

Cauliflower and gravy can be prepared a day ahead and refrigerated. Let cauliflower come to room temperature and warm gravy before assembling for baking.

◆ *Preheat oven to 350°F (180°C)*
◆ *13-by 9-inch (3 L) baking dish*

1	medium cauliflower (about 1 1/2 lbs/750 g)	1
3 tbsp	vegetable oil, divided	45 mL
2 cups	finely chopped onions (2 to 3)	500 mL
2 tsp	minced green chilies, preferably serranos	10 mL
1 tsp	minced peeled gingerroot	5 mL
1 tsp	minced garlic	5 mL
1 cup	finely chopped tomato or 1 can (14 oz/398 mL) diced tomatoes, liquid reserved	250 mL
1 1/2 tsp	coriander powder	7 mL
3/4 tsp	cumin powder	4 mL
1/2 tsp	turmeric	2 mL
1 1/2 tsp	salt or to taste	7 mL
2 tbsp	coarsely chopped garlic	25 mL

1. Remove leaves from cauliflower. In a large saucepan filled with about 3 inches (7.5 cm) water, place cauliflower, stem side down. Cover and bring to a boil over medium–high heat. Reduce heat to medium and cook for 2 minutes. Remove from heat and let stand, covered, for 3 minutes longer to steam. Remove cauliflower carefully from water and place in a colander under cool running water to stop further cooking. Set aside to drain. Cauliflower should be tender-crisp.

2. Meanwhile, in a small saucepan, heat 2 tbsp (25 mL) of the oil over medium–high heat. Sauté onions until golden, about 10 minutes.

3. Stir in chilies, ginger and garlic. Reduce heat to medium and continue to cook until onions are browned, 5 to 8 minutes longer.

4. Mix in tomatoes or drained canned tomatoes, reserving liquid. Cook until tomatoes can be mashed with back of spoon, about 5 minutes.

5. Stir in coriander, cumin, turmeric and salt. Cook for 2 to 3 minutes. If using fresh tomatoes, add ¾ cup (175 mL) water; if canned, add reserved tomato liquid. Reduce heat to low. Cover and simmer for 10 minutes. Gravy should be thick.

6. Place cauliflower in baking dish. Spoon gravy in between florets, taking care cauliflower does not break apart. Cover completely with remaining gravy. Bake in preheated oven until cauliflower is tender, about 20 minutes.

7. In a small saucepan, heat remaining oil over medium heat. Sauté garlic until golden, about 2 minutes. Pour on top of cauliflower just before serving.

8. Serve either in baking dish or transfer carefully, without breaking, to a serving platter.

Indian Macaroni and Cheese

Macaroni and cheese is a culinary legacy of the Raj, but as was usual, the dish took on Indian overtones. So though the original still survives, an Indian version also shows up on menus.

❄

* *Preheat oven to 375°F (190°C)*
* *4-cup (1 L) baking dish, sprayed with vegetable spray*

1 tbsp	vegetable oil	15 mL
1 tsp	cumin seeds	5 mL
2 tsp	minced peeled gingerroot	10 mL
2 tsp	minced garlic	10 mL
1 ½ cups	chopped onions (about 2)	375 mL
3 cups	chopped Roma tomatoes (4 to 6)	750 mL
½ tsp	salt or to taste	2 mL
2 tbsp	butter	25 mL
3 tbsp	all-purpose flour	45 mL
1 cup	milk, warmed	250 mL
½ cup	shredded Cheddar cheese, divided	125 mL
½ to 1 tsp	cayenne pepper (optional)	2 to 5 mL
1 cup	elbow macaroni, cooked	250 mL
1	tomato, sliced	1

1. In a saucepan, heat oil over medium heat. Sauté cumin, ginger and garlic for 1 minute. Add onions and cook until translucent, 6 to 8 minutes.

2. Add tomatoes and salt. Mix well. Cook, covered, over medium–low heat until tomatoes break down, 5 to 7 minutes. Mash with back of spoon. Set aside.

3. In another saucepan, melt butter over medium–low heat. Remove from heat and whisk in flour. Add milk in a slow stream, whisking continuously to make a smooth mixture. Return to medium heat and cook, stirring continuously, until sauce is thick, 5 to 7 minutes.

4. Stir in ¼ cup (50 mL) of the cheese until melted. Stir in cayenne pepper, if using. Add tomato masala and mix well. Stir in macaroni.

5. Pour mixture into prepared dish. Arrange tomato slices on top. Sprinkle remaining cheese evenly on top.

6. Bake in preheated oven until top is bubbly and lightly browned, 25 to 30 minutes.

Vegetables

JULIA CHILD ONCE said that if she had to become a vegetarian, Indian food is what she would eat. I agree with her. There is no doubt that we have a way with vegetables that transforms the most mundane into something extraordinary. I like to say that vegetables replace meat as the most important food group in our diet, and in most cases, the recipes are very quick and easy to prepare.

Spices enhance most food, but the key is to use them judiciously. Often less is more, as in the recipe Carrots with Cumin and Nigella. Other times, simple spices transform an everyday vegetable into an astonishing taste treat, as in Sweet-and-Spicy Butternut Squash. In any event, I would urge you to buy seasonal vegetables, preferably locally grown whenever possible.

A quick word about frozen vegetables. When a particular vegetable is not as fresh as I like, I prefer to opt for frozen. In most cases, vegetables are quick-frozen as they are harvested in the fields; with modern processing technology, there is no loss of flavor or nutrients. Using frozen vegetables is also a great time-saver.

❋   ❋   ❋

Lower-Fat Panir

Panir, the only form of cheese indigenous to India, is very popular in Punjab. This recipe is one I developed when I was looking for a lower-fat version that was still as good as the original full-fat one. I have taught this recipe for almost 20 years and have always received raves. Panir can be grated and used as a stuffing for vegetables and patties, diced and simmered in vegetable curries, and cut into batons and stir-fried with vegetables.

❋

TIP

Panir can be wrapped in plastic wrap and refrigerated for up to 4 days or frozen, tightly wrapped, for up to 3 months.

◆ *Double layer of fine cheesecloth*

8 cups	2% milk	2 L
4 cups	buttermilk	1 L

1. Line a large strainer with a double layer of cheesecloth.

2. In a large saucepan or enamel pot over medium heat, bring milk to a boil. (Do not use a nonstick pan.)

3. Pour in buttermilk and stir. When liquid separates from solids in about 1 minute, remove from heat. Stir until solids are completely separated.

4. Pour contents of pan into cheesecloth-lined strainer. Discard liquid or save for another use.

5. Gather up ends of cheesecloth, twist to form a ball and tie with string. Tie the ends loosely on kitchen faucet to drain over sink for 5 minutes. Open cheesecloth, flatten panir with hand and enclose again.

6. Place a tray at edge of sink. Place wrapped panir on tray and twist ends of cheesecolth arranging both ends to drip over the edge into sink. Place a weight on top of panir. (You can use the pot in which panir was made and fill three-quarters full of water.) Let drain for 30 minutes or longer. (Panir will be solid at this point. The range in time is just to indicate that it is not critical to remove at 30 minutes, but okay to leave longer.) Remove and use as required.

Creamy Broccoli Curry

Serves 8

Here's a delicious way to get a broccoli boost. The vegetable is well suited to Indian seasonings and cooking techniques. Substituting buttermilk (see Variation, below) for the yogurt and water adds a little tang, which I prefer.

❋

VARIATION

Replace yogurt and 1 cup (250 mL) water with 2 cups (500 mL) buttermilk. Stir together chickpea flour and ¼ cup (50 mL) water until smooth. Stir mixture into buttermilk. Pour into broccoli purée in Step 4.

2 tbsp	vegetable oil	25 mL
1 cup	chopped onion	250 mL
1 tbsp	minced green chilies, preferably serranos	15 mL
1 tsp	minced peeled gingerroot	5 mL
1 tsp	minced garlic	5 mL
3 cups	finely chopped broccoli	750 mL
1 tsp	coriander powder	5 mL
½ tsp	cayenne pepper	2 mL
½ tsp	turmeric	2 mL
⅓ to ½ cup	milk or water (optional)	75 to 125 mL
1 cup	plain nonfat yogurt	250 mL
2 tbsp	chickpea flour (besan)	25 mL
1 tsp	salt or to taste	5 mL

1. In a saucepan, heat oil over medium–high heat. Sauté onion until beginning to turn golden, 6 to 8 minutes.

2. Reduce heat to medium. Stir in chilies, ginger and garlic and sauté for 2 minutes. Add broccoli, coriander, cayenne and turmeric. Mix well and sauté for 3 to 4 minutes. Remove from heat and let cool slightly.

3. In a blender, purée mixture, adding a little milk or water if necessary for blending. Return to saucepan.

4. Whisk together yogurt, chickpea flour, 1 cup (250 mL) water and salt, making sure to remove all lumps. Pour into broccoli purée. Reduce heat to medium-low. Mix well and bring to a gentle boil. Cook, uncovered, until curry thickens, 6 to 8 minutes.

5. Serve with rice or an Indian bread.

Mustard Seed Potatoes

I estimate I have a repertoire of more than 35 recipes featuring potatoes, and this is probably my favorite. It is a classic "dry fry" style of cooking vegetables: it uses a technique referred to as "dum" cooking, which allows the inherent moisture in the vegetable to create steam, condense and cook the vegetable until tender. Besides their outstanding taste, the potatoes are beautiful: a riot of spice colors coats the potatoes, which are flecked with dark mustard seeds and the confetti of cilantro.

❋

◆ *Large wok or heavy skillet with lid*

2 tbsp	vegetable oil	25 mL
2 tsp	mustard seeds	10 mL
2 lbs	thin-skinned potatoes, unpeeled, cut into 1-inch (2.5 cm) pieces	1 kg
1 tbsp	sliced green chilies, preferably serranos	15 mL
1 1/2 tsp	coriander powder	7 mL
1 tsp	cayenne pepper	5 mL
3/4 tsp	turmeric	4 mL
1 1/2 tsp	salt or to taste	7 mL
3 tbsp	grated unsweetened fresh or frozen coconut (optional)	45 mL
1/3 cup	cilantro, chopped	75 mL

1. In a heavy skillet, heat oil over high heat until a couple of mustard seeds thrown in start to sputter. Add remaining mustard seeds and cover quickly.

2. When the seeds stop popping within a few seconds, uncover and reduce heat to medium. Add potatoes, chilies, coriander, cayenne pepper, turmeric and salt. Mix well. Reduce heat to low. Cover tightly and cook until potatoes are tender, 12 to 15 minutes. Stir every 5 minutes to prevent sticking. Sprinkle with 1 tbsp (15 mL) water at a time, if necessary, to prevent burning. Some potatoes will be randomly crispy.

3. Remove from heat and sprinkle with grated coconut, if using, and cilantro. Serve with an Indian bread.

Three-Seed Potatoes

Serves 8

This simple dish packs crunch and flavor and can be served hot or at room temperature. It is an excellent accompaniment to non-Indian entrées and makes great picnic fare, too.

TIP

Maintaining the correct heat level is important. There should be an audible sizzle, indicating that the potatoes are cooking and not just on warm. Try not to lift the lid more than once because the built-up steam is necessary to cook the potatoes.

◆ *Large wok or skillet with lid*

2 lbs	new or other thin-skinned potatoes, cut into 1-inch (2.5 cm) pieces	1 kg
2 tbsp	vegetable oil	25 mL
1 tbsp	cumin seeds	15 mL
2 tbsp	sesame seeds	25 mL
1 tsp	nigella seeds (kalaunji)	5 mL
1 tsp	salt or to taste	5 mL
½ tsp	cayenne pepper	2 mL
3 to 4 tbsp	lemon juice	45 to 60 mL

1. In a large saucepan, cover potatoes with water and bring to boil over medium-high heat. Cook until almost tender, 6 to 8 minutes. Drain well.

2. In a large wok or skillet, heat oil over medium–high heat. Add cumin seeds and stir-fry for a few seconds before adding sesame seeds. Stir-fry for a few more seconds, then add nigella seeds. Add potatoes, salt and cayenne pepper. Toss well until seeds coat potatoes.

3. Reduce heat to medium. Cover and cook potatoes, stirring once, until slightly crusty, 12 to 15 minutes.

4. Remove from heat and toss potatoes with lemon juice to taste.

Methi Aloo

Potatoes with Fenugreek Leaves

Serves 6 to 8

Fenugreek leaves and seeds are used extensively in Indian cooking. Fenugreek has a bitter, strong flavor but translates into mouth-watering recipes. It is one of the few herbs that is very flavorful even when used dried.

❋

TIP

If using dried leaves, rinse in mesh strainer before using.

4 tbsp	vegetable oil, divided	60 mL
2	dried red Indian chilies	2
¾ tsp	fenugreek seeds (methi)	4 mL
1 cup	chopped onion	250 mL
4 cups	fresh fenugreek leaves (methi), washed and chopped, or ¼ cup (50 mL) dried fenugreek leaves (kasoori methi) (see Tip, left)	1 L
2 lbs	thin-skinned potatoes, cut into 1-inch (2.5 cm) pieces	1 kg
2 tsp	salt or to taste	10 mL
	Juice of 1 lemon (optional)	

1. In a large skillet, heat 2 tbsp (25 mL) of the oil over medium heat. Sauté chilies and fenugreek seeds until slightly darker, about 30 seconds.

2. Add onion and sauté until golden, 5 to 7 minutes.

3. Add fenugreek leaves and sauté until incorporated, about 2 minutes. Remove from heat and set aside.

4. In the same skillet, heat remaining oil over medium-high heat. Sauté potatoes for 2 minutes. Sprinkle with salt. Cover and reduce heat to medium-low. Cook, undisturbed, for 6 to 8 minutes to brown potatoes. Stir and continue in the same manner until potatoes are cooked and well browned, 6 to 8 minutes longer. Stir in onion mixture and heat through. Add lemon juice, if using. Serve with an Indian bread.

Hena's Finger Potatoes

Delicious potatoes, which make a marvelous marriage with any kind of barbecued meat or fried chicken, are just as wonderful by themselves. An old friend who is renowned for her cuisine gave me this recipe when visiting from India.

✻

TIPS

I like to serve these to accompany beer.

◆

To toast sesame seeds: Spread in a dry skillet and toast on medium heat until starting to color, 3 to 4 minutes. Shake pan periodically to toast evenly. Seeds will turn slightly darker as they cool.

4 tsp	vegetable oil, divided	20 mL
1/4 cup	raw cashews, broken into large pieces	50 mL
1/4 cup	raisins	50 mL
2 lbs	all-purpose potatoes, peeled and cut into 1/2-inch (1 cm) thick fries	1 kg
2 tsp	hot pepper flakes or to taste	10 mL
1 tsp	cumin powder	5 mL
2 tsp	salt or to taste	10 mL
1 tsp	mango powder (amchur) (optional)	5 mL
2 tbsp	sesame seeds, toasted (see Tips, left)	25 mL

1. In a large nonstick skillet, heat 2 tsp (10 mL) of the oil over medium heat. Sauté cashews and raisins until cashews are golden and raisins are plump, about 2 minutes. Remove with slotted spoon and set aside.

2. In the same skillet, heat remaining oil. Stir-fry potatoes to coat with oil. Spread in a single layer and cover. Cook over medium heat, without stirring, for 5 to 7 minutes. Stir and spread into single layer again. Cover and continue to cook, adjusting heat to brown potatoes without burning, for 6 to 8 minutes longer. There should be a golden crust on most potatoes when done.

3. Sprinkle with hot pepper flakes, cumin, salt and mango powder, if using. Add reserved cashews and raisins and sesame seeds. Toss well and adjust seasonings. Serve as a side dish or as finger food.

Stir-Fried Okra
with Tomatoes

*Okra is very popular
throughout India and is
available year-round.
This is the okra recipe
that was prepared most
often in our home and
is still a favorite. The
technique of stir-frying
eliminates the
"sliminess" associated
with okra and results
in soft but firm pieces.*

❋

TIP

Mango powder is sour
and astringent. It is
ground sun-dried
unripened mango.

2 tbsp	vegetable oil	25 mL
4 to 5	Roma tomatoes, cut into ½-inch (1 cm) wedges (about 3 cups/750 mL)	4 to 5
2 tsp	coriander powder	10 mL
1½ tsp	cumin powder	7 mL
¾ tsp	turmeric	4 mL
½ tsp	cayenne pepper	2 mL
1 tsp	salt or to taste	5 mL
1½ lbs	okra, cut into ½-inch (1 cm) pieces	750 g
2	medium potatoes, cut into ½-inch (1 cm) dice	2
	Freshly ground black pepper to taste	
1 tsp	mango powder (amchur) or 1½ tbsp (22 mL) freshly squeezed lemon juice	5 mL

1. In a large skillet with a tight-fitting lid, heat oil over medium heat. Add tomatoes and sauté until soft and mushy, 4 to 5 minutes. Mash with back of spoon.

2. Add coriander, cumin, turmeric, cayenne and salt. Sauté, stirring continuously, for 2 minutes.

3. Add okra and potatoes and mix well. Reduce heat slightly and sauté until okra is no longer sticky, about 5 minutes.

4. Sprinkle okra mixture with 1 tbsp (15 mL) water. Reduce heat to low. Cover and cook, stirring once to prevent sticking, until softened, 8 to 10 minutes.

5. Remove from heat. Sprinkle with pepper and mango powder.

Green Beans
with Mustard Seeds

Serves 6 to 8

I have cooked this dish — a family recipe — for more than 40 years. It is excellent as a side dish to chicken, fish and pork entrées.

TIP

Make sure that there is an audible sizzle at all times to indicate that vegetables are cooking.

2 tbsp	vegetable oil	25 mL
1½ tsp	mustard seeds	7 mL
1½ lbs	green beans, fresh or frozen, cut into ½-inch (1 cm) pieces	750 g
3	medium potatoes, cut into ½-inch (1 cm) cubes (unpeeled if thin-skinned)	3
1½ tsp	coriander powder	7 mL
¾ tsp	turmeric	4 mL
½ tsp	cayenne pepper	2 mL
1½ tsp	salt or to taste	7 mL

1. In a large skillet with a tight-fitting lid, heat oil over high heat until a couple of mustard seeds thrown in start to sputter. Add remaining mustard seeds and cover quickly.

2. When seeds stop popping in a few seconds, uncover and reduce heat to medium. Add green beans and potatoes.

3. Sprinkle mixture with coriander, turmeric, cayenne and salt. Mix well. Sprinkle with 1 tbsp (15 mL) water. Reduce heat to low (see Tip, left). Cover and cook, stirring once to prevent sticking, until vegetables are tender, about 10 minutes.

Green Beans and Carrots with Aromatic Spices

This is not your everyday green bean and carrot mix. Flash-fried whole seeds infuse this all-American vegetable combination and turn it into an exotic dish. It's also great as a salad, chilled or at room temperature.

❀

2 tbsp	vegetable oil	25 mL
1 tsp	mustard seeds	5 mL
1 tsp	cumin seeds	5 mL
1 tbsp	minced garlic	15 mL
1 tbsp	minced green chilies, preferably serranos	15 mL
1/4 cup	coarsely crushed roasted peanuts	50 mL
1/4 cup	grated unsweetened fresh or frozen coconut, divided	50 mL
1/2 tsp	turmeric	2 mL
1/2 tsp	cayenne pepper	2 mL
8 oz	green beans, cut into 2-inch (5 cm) sections	250 g
8 oz	carrots, peeled and sliced diagonally 1/4 inch (0.5 cm) thick (2 to 3)	250 g
1 tsp	salt or to taste	5 mL

1. In a large skillet with a tight-fitting lid, heat oil over high heat until a couple of mustard seeds thrown in start to sputter. Add remaining mustard seeds and cover quickly.

2. When seeds stop popping in a few seconds, uncover, reduce heat to medium and add cumin seeds. Sauté for 30 seconds. Add garlic, chilies, peanuts and 3 tbsp (45 mL) of the coconut. Reduce heat slightly to prevent burning and stir-fry for 2 minutes. Add turmeric and cayenne. Sauté for 1 minute longer (add 1 1/2 tsp/7 mL water if necessary). Do not allow masala to burn.

3. Stir in beans and carrots. Add salt and mix well. Sprinkle with 1 tbsp (15 mL) water. Cover and cook over medium heat for 5 minutes. Reduce heat to low and stir. Cook, covered, until vegetables are tender, 5 to 8 minutes.

4. Garnish with remaining coconut to serve.

Carrots with Cumin and Nigella

Serves 8

Nigella seeds have a distinctive flavor — there is no substitute. They are always used whole.

2 tbsp	vegetable oil	25 mL
1 1/2 tsp	cumin seeds	7 mL
1 tsp	nigella seeds (kalaunji)	5 mL
2 tsp	minced green chilies, preferably serranos	10 mL
2 tsp	minced peeled gingerroot	10 mL
4 cups	grated peeled carrots (about 1 lb/500 g)	1 L
3/4 tsp	turmeric	4 mL
1 tsp	granulated sugar	5 mL
1/2 tsp	salt or to taste	2 mL
2 tbsp	lime or lemon juice	25 mL

1. In a skillet, heat oil over medium heat. Add cumin and nigella seeds and sauté for 1 minute. Add chilies and ginger and stir-fry for 1 minute.

2. Add carrots, turmeric, sugar and salt. Reduce heat to low. Sauté until carrots are softened, 4 to 5 minutes.

3. Mix in lime juice and serve.

Sweet-and-Spicy Butternut Squash

Pumpkin is very popular in India and is available year-round. Butternut squash is similar, and I use it as an excellent substitute. It is highly nutritious and tasty, too.

❋

TIP

Jaggery is unrefined cane sugar and has essential vitamins and minerals. It has a rich taste very similar to molasses.

3 to 3½ lbs	butternut squash	1.5 to 1.75 kg
2 tbsp	vegetable oil	25 mL
1 tsp	fenugreek seeds (methi)	5 mL
2 tbsp	coriander powder	25 mL
¾ tsp	asafetida (hing)	4 mL
¾ tsp	cayenne pepper	4 mL
1 tsp	salt or to taste	5 mL
3 tbsp	jaggery (gur) (see Tip, left) or dark brown sugar	45 mL
2 tsp	mango powder (amchur) or 2 tbsp (25 mL) freshly squeezed lemon juice	10 mL

1. With a sharp knife, cut squash in half lengthwise through stem end. Remove seeds and fibers. Peel each half and cut into ½-inch (1 cm) cubes.

2. In a large saucepan, heat oil over medium heat. Add fenugreek and sauté for several seconds until lightly browned. Stir in coriander, asafetida and cayenne pepper. Stir for a few seconds, then add squash. Add salt and mix well to coat squash with spices.

3. Reduce heat to medium-low. Cook, covered, until tender, about 15 minutes. Squash should not get too mushy.

4. Stir in jaggery and mango powder and cook for 2 to 3 minutes to melt jaggery and to coat squash.

Bell Peppers with Roasted Chickpea Flour

My Gujerati friend in Houston, a consultant on all things to do with Gujerati cuisine — which has long been recognized as the fount of outstanding vegetarian fare — shared this recipe with me several years ago. I know you will enjoy it as much as I do.

✿

TIP

As the peppers cook down, they exude juices that combine with the chickpea flour to make a wonderful coating.

¹/₂ cup	chickpea flour (besan)	125 mL
4 lbs	green bell peppers or mix of colors (8 to 10)	2 kg
¹/₄ cup	vegetable oil	50 mL
4 tsp	coriander powder	20 mL
2 tsp	cumin powder	10 mL
1 tsp	turmeric	5 mL
1 tsp	cayenne pepper	5 mL
1 tsp	salt	5 mL
1 tsp	granulated sugar	5 mL
¹/₄ cup	coarsely crushed roasted peanuts (optional)	50 mL

1. In a heavy skillet over low heat, toast chickpea flour, stirring constantly to prevent burning, until lightly browned and aromatic, 3 to 4 minutes. Set aside.

2. Cut bell peppers into 1¹/₂-inch (4 cm) pieces, discarding stems, seeds and membranes.

3. In a large saucepan, heat oil over medium–high heat. Sauté peppers until softened, 6 to 8 minutes.

4. Reduce heat to medium. Add coriander, cumin, turmeric, cayenne pepper, salt and sugar. Mix well. Sauté for 2 minutes longer. Sprinkle chickpea flour on top of peppers. Do not mix.

5. Reduce heat to low. Cook, covered, until peppers are very soft, 6 to 8 minutes. Stir to mix. Remove from heat and sprinkle with crushed peanuts, if using.

Cauliflower and Potatoes with Ginger and Chilies

	Serves 8	

Both a restaurant favorite and a popular dish in north Indian homes, this recipe is the epitome of simplicity. It is a staple in my home, particularly when I am pressed for time.

TIP

This is wonderful as a filling for a pita sandwich or for a flavorful wrap. It is typical of the foods Indians like to pack for a picnic.

♦ *Large wok or skillet with tight-fitting lid*

¼ cup	vegetable oil	50 mL
1½ tsp	cumin seeds	7 mL
3 tbsp	coarsely chopped peeled gingerroot	45 mL
2 tbsp	minced green chilies, preferably serranos	25 mL
1 tsp	turmeric	5 mL
¾ tsp	cayenne pepper	4 mL
1	medium cauliflower, cut into 1½-inch (4 cm) florets (about 1½ lbs/750 g)	1
2 to 3	potatoes, cut into 1½-inch (4 cm) pieces	2 to 3
1½ tsp	salt or to taste	7 mL
3 to 4 tbsp	cilantro, chopped, for garnish	45 to 60 mL

1. In a large wok or skillet, heat oil over medium heat. Add cumin seeds and sauté until slightly darker, about 1 minute. Add ginger and chilies. Stir-fry for 2 minutes.

2. Stir in turmeric and cayenne pepper. Stir-fry for 30 seconds. Add cauliflower, potatoes and salt. Mix well. Cover with a tight-fitting lid and cook on medium-low heat until vegetables are tender, 10 to 12 minutes. Stir gently occasionally, taking care not to break florets.

3. Garnish with cilantro and serve with an Indian bread.

Cauliflower Peas Keema

Serves 8

Keema is the Hindi word for ground meat. Here, cauliflower is chopped into very small pieces to resemble ground meat — hence the name. This makes a wonderful filling for a pita sandwich with yogurt topping.

TIP

Double the recipe and freeze the rest in an airtight container for up to 3 months. It is a delicious stuffing or topping for baked potatoes with a dollop of yogurt on top. Stir into leftover rice and serve with a yogurt salad.

2 tbsp	vegetable oil	25 mL
1 1/2 tsp	cumin seeds	7 mL
1 tbsp	minced green chilies, preferably serranos	15 mL
1 tsp	minced peeled gingerroot	5 mL
1 tsp	minced garlic	5 mL
1 cup	finely chopped onion	250 mL
2 cups	chopped tomatoes	500 mL
1 1/2 tsp	salt or to taste	7 mL
1 1/2 tsp	coriander powder	7 mL
1/2 tsp	cayenne pepper	2 mL
1/2 tsp	turmeric	2 mL
4 cups	finely chopped cauliflower	1 L
1 cup	frozen peas, thawed	250 mL
3 tbsp	cilantro, chopped, for garnish	45 mL

1. In a large skillet, heat oil over medium heat. Add cumin seeds and sauté for 1 minute. Add chilies, ginger and garlic. Sauté for 1 minute.
2. Add onion and sauté until golden, 6 to 8 minutes.
3. Add tomatoes and salt. Cook until softened, 6 to 8 minutes. Mash with back of a spoon. Add coriander, cayenne pepper and turmeric. Cook for 2 minutes.
4. Add cauliflower and peas. Mix well. Reduce heat to low. Cook, covered, until tender, 5 to 10 minutes. Sprinkle with cilantro and serve with an Indian bread.

Preeti's Cabbage with Peanuts

With its jewel-like colors, this dish is as much a treat for the eyes as it is for the palate. Quick and easy to prepare, it can accompany any entrée, Indian or otherwise.

❋

TIP

Once cooled, this dish can be covered and set aside at room temperature for up to 6 hours. Reheating is not necessary. If making ahead, do not add peanuts until ready to serve.

• *Large wok or skillet with tight-fitting lid*

2 tbsp	vegetable oil	25 mL
1 1/2 tsp	mustard seeds	7 mL
25 to 30	fresh curry leaves (optional)	25 to 30
3 to 4	green chilies, preferably serranos, cut into 3/4-inch (2 cm) pieces	3 to 4
8 cups	finely sliced cabbage	2 L
3/4 cup	finely sliced red or green bell pepper	175 mL
3/4 tsp	salt or to taste	4 mL
1/3 cup	skinned raw peanuts, dry roasted in skillet	75 mL

1. In a large wok or skillet, heat oil over high heat until a couple of mustard seeds thrown in start to sputter. Add remaining mustard seeds and cover quickly.

2. When the seeds stop popping in a few seconds, uncover, reduce heat to medium and add curry leaves, if using, and chilies. Sauté for 30 seconds.

3. Add cabbage, bell pepper and salt. Stir-fry until cabbage is softened, 3 to 4 minutes.

4. Fold in peanuts and cook for 1 minute.

Sweet, Sour and Spicy Eggplant

	Serves 8	

This is eggplant with a sour twist. The fabulous flavors come through brilliantly. If you like eggplant, don't miss this easy recipe.

❋

1	eggplant (about 1 1/2 lbs/750 g)	1
3	medium potatoes, preferably thin-skinned	3
2 tbsp	vegetable oil	25 mL
1 1/2 tsp	cumin seeds	7 mL
1 tsp	minced peeled gingerroot	5 mL
1 tsp	minced garlic	5 mL
2 tsp	coriander powder	10 mL
3/4 tsp	turmeric	4 mL
3/4 tsp	cayenne pepper	4 mL
1 1/2 tsp	salt or to taste	7 mL
2 1/2 tsp	granulated sugar	12 mL
1/3 cup	white vinegar	75 mL

1. Cut eggplant (do not peel) into pieces 1 inch (2.5 cm) thick and 3 inches (7.5 cm) long. If potatoes are thin-skinned, cut (do not peel) into same size.

2. In a nonstick skillet, heat oil over medium heat. Add cumin seeds and sauté for 1 minute. Stir in ginger and garlic and sauté for 1 minute.

3. Add eggplant, potatoes, coriander, turmeric, cayenne and salt. Mix well. Cover and reduce heat to low and cook until vegetables are tender, 10 to 12 minutes. (Shake pan occasionally to prevent sticking.) If necessary, add 2 tbsp (25 mL) water to deglaze pan partway through cooking.

4. Stir sugar into vinegar to dissolve. Pour over vegetables and toss gently to coat. Cook, covered, until vinegar is absorbed, about 2 minutes.

5. Serve with an Indian bread or pita bread.

Stuffed Eggplant

Delicate Japanese eggplant stuffed with a spiced onion filling can be served as a side dish or placed on top of rice to infuse it with amazing flavors and taste.

TIP

To toast seeds:
Place mustard and poppy seeds in a small heavy dry skillet and toast over medium heat for 3 to 4 minutes. Shake skillet occasionally to prevent burning. Grind to a powder with rolling pin, mortar and pestle, or spice grinder.

2 lbs	Japanese eggplant	1 kg
1	medium onion	1
1	piece peeled gingerroot, ½ inch (1 cm) long	1
4	cloves garlic	4
1	green chili, preferably serrano	1
6 to 8	mint leaves	6 to 8
2 tbsp	cilantro, chopped	25 mL
1 tbsp	coriander powder	15 mL
½ tsp	turmeric	2 mL
½ tsp	cumin powder	2 mL
1 tsp	poppy seeds, toasted and powdered (see Tip, left)	5 mL
1 tsp	mustard seeds, toasted and powdered (see Tip, left)	5 mL
3 tbsp	Thai tamarind paste	45 mL
1¼ tsp	salt or to taste	6 mL
2 tbsp	vegetable oil	25 mL

1. Cut eggplant into 3-inch (7.5 cm) lengths. Cut an "X" in each piece starting on one cut side to within ½ inch (1 cm) of bottom. (There will be 2 cut sides on some pieces, depending on the length of eggplant.)

2. In a food processor, purée onion, ginger, garlic, chili, mint and cilantro. Add coriander powder, turmeric, cumin, poppy and mustard seeds, tamarind paste and salt. Process to mix. Transfer to a bowl. Mixture will be slightly runny. Using a small spoon, stuff mixture into slits in eggplant.

3. In a large nonstick skillet, heat oil over medium heat. Carefully place eggplant in skillet in single layer. (These are long pieces like a roll. Lay lengthwise so they are easy to roll in skillet to cook evenly.) Reduce heat to medium-low and cook, covered, for 5 minutes. Turn once and continue to cook until tender, 8 to 10 minutes, shaking pan occasionally to prevent sticking.

Onion and Potato Sauté

This is the type of dish that is thrown together in a hurry when unexpected guests come to visit close to mealtime — Indian hospitality expects that they be invited to stay. Add to this some scrumptious fritters and perhaps an egg curry, and an impromptu feast appears at short notice.

❈

TIP

I call this dish Indian Hash Browns. They are perfect to serve for brunch with any style of eggs.

2 to 3 tbsp	vegetable oil	25 to 45 mL
1 1/2 tsp	cumin seeds	7 mL
2	whole dried red Indian chilies	2
1 1/2 lbs	thin-skinned potatoes, unpeeled, sliced 1/4 inch (0.5 cm) thick	750 g
1 lb	yellow onions, cut into 1/4-inch (0.5 cm) thick rings	500 g
1 1/2 tsp	coriander powder	7 mL
1/2 tsp	cayenne pepper	2 mL
1/2 tsp	turmeric	2 mL
1 1/2 tsp	salt or to taste	7 mL

1. In a large nonstick skillet, heat oil over medium heat. Add cumin seeds and chilies. Stir-fry for 1 minute.

2. Scatter potatoes and onions in skillet. Sprinkle coriander, cayenne pepper, turmeric and salt evenly on top. Toss to mix. Spread in a layer, cover with tight-fitting lid and cook over medium heat until there is a sizzle. Reduce heat to medium-low. Cook, stirring occasionally to prevent sticking, until vegetables are tender, 12 to 14 minutes. Correct heat is important, and there should be an audible sizzle at all times to indicate vegetables are cooking and not just on warm.

Zucchini with Five Seeds

Serves 8

The amazing flavors of five flash-fried seeds are the only spices in this light summer dish. Perfect for when gardens overflow with zucchini and tomatoes.

❋

2 tsp	vegetable oil	10 mL
1/2 tsp	crushed coriander seeds	2 mL
1/2 tsp	mustard seeds	2 mL
1/2 tsp	cumin seeds	2 mL
1/2 tsp	nigella seeds (kalaunji)	2 mL
1/4 tsp	fenugreek seeds (methi)	1 mL
2	whole dried red Indian chilies	2
2 cups	diced onions (1/2-inch/1 cm dice)	500 mL
6 cups	diced zucchini (1/2-inch/1 cm dice) (about 1 1/2 lbs/750 g)	1.5 L
1 tsp	salt or to taste	5 mL
1 1/2 cups	chopped tomatoes (2 to 3)	375 mL

1. In a large saucepan, heat oil over medium–high heat. Add coriander, mustard, cumin, nigella and fenugreek seeds and chilies. Sauté until seeds darken, about 30 seconds.

2. Add onion and sauté until soft, 3 to 4 minutes.

3. Add zucchini and salt and mix well. Add 1/2 cup (125 mL) water. Cover, reduce heat to medium–low and simmer until vegetables are tender, 6 to 8 minutes.

4. Add tomatoes and cook, uncovered, for 2 to 3 minutes longer. Tomatoes should be soft, not mushy.

Raitas and Chutneys

RAITA (PRONOUNCED "RYE-TA") is yogurt salad and is an essential element of the Indian menu. Yogurt is an ancient Indian food. It is nutritious and considered to be a healing and soothing food that cools the body — particularly welcome in the summer. Most raitas can be made up to a day ahead, and leftovers are good for three to four days. I think of raita as a palate cleanser and "cooler-offer" for spicy dishes, calming mouths that seem to be on fire. I have found that using lower-fat or nonfat yogurt does not change the texture of raitas, so any type is acceptable. Even today, Indians almost always make their own fresh yogurt, a nightly ritual that is followed like clockwork. Milk is brought to a boil, cooled to lukewarm, a spoonful of yogurt saved from the previous day is stirred in and the warm milk is poured into a bowl. It is covered and left overnight in a warm spot. In the morning, the bowl is put in the refrigerator to chill and firm up.

Condiments such as pickles and chutneys are a must on an Indian table as they allow us to customize our food. Pickles are very often store-bought; they are pungent, salty and need to be used with discretion. A teaspoonful per diner is all you need; a tiny taste is included with each mouthful. Chutneys are the equivalent of dips and relishes and can be sweet and cooked. The most popular is mango chutney. Fresh ingredients can also be puréed together to make a tasty mixture that is used as a dip or a spread. The one that comes to mind immediately is the ubiquitous "green chutney," a purée of cilantro, mint and seasonings.

Included here are some easy, versatile and very tasty recipes that I hope will encourage you to experiment further.

❋ ❋ ❋

Angoor Raita
Cilantro and Mint Yogurt with Grapes

One of my food-loving friends travels with her notebook to jot down recipes at short notice. One summer day, she visited and made this amazing raita for us. I was surprised at the results.

4 cups	plain yogurt, divided	1 L
1/2 cup	cilantro leaves	125 mL
1/3 cup	mint leaves	75 mL
2 to 3	green chilies, preferably serranos	2 to 3
1 1/2 cups	seedless grapes	375 mL
1/2 tsp	salt or to taste	2 mL

1. In a blender, combine 1/4 cup (50 mL) yogurt, cilantro, mint and chilies to make a smooth paste. Transfer to a bowl.

2. Stir in remaining yogurt until smooth and creamy. Stir in grapes and salt.

3. Cover and chill well before serving. (Can be refrigerated for up to 3 days.)

Caramelized Carrot Pudding
(Gajar ka Halwa) (page 179)

Beet and Potato Raita

Try this raita with grilled foods. It provides a cool, colorful contrast.

❀

TIP

Make this colorful raita for a holiday buffet table.

1 cup	plain yogurt	250 mL
½ cup	diced cooked potatoes	125 mL
1 tbsp	finely sliced green onions	15 mL
½ tsp	salt or to taste	2 mL
¼ tsp	freshly ground black pepper or to taste	1 mL
½ cup	diced cooked beets or drained canned beets	125 mL
	Finely sliced green onion tops	

1. Stir yogurt in a bowl until smooth and creamy. Stir in potatoes, onions, salt and pepper. Cover and chill well before serving. (Can be refrigerated for up to 24 hours.)

2. Stir in beets just before serving to prevent beets from turning yogurt deep red. Garnish with green onions.

Mango Lassi (page 183)

Kakri Raita
Cucumber Raita

Serves 8

This is arguably the most recognized raita, available on every restaurant menu. Its simplicity also makes it a favorite of home cooks.

TIP

To toast cumin seeds: Spread in a single layer in a dry heavy skillet over medium heat. Stir periodically until there is an aroma and seeds are a few shades darker, 3 to 4 minutes. Remove from heat and grind in a spice grinder.

1 cup	plain yogurt	250 mL
2 cups	diced cucumber	500 mL
2 tbsp	cilantro, chopped	25 mL
1 tbsp	chopped mint	15 mL
1/2 tsp	cumin powder, preferably fresh roasted and ground (see Tip, left)	2 mL
	Salt and freshly ground black pepper to taste	

1. Stir yogurt in a bowl until smooth and creamy. Stir in cucumber, cilantro, mint and cumin. Season with salt and pepper.
2. Cover and chill well before serving. (Can be refrigerated for up 24 hours.)

Tomato Raita

Serves 4

The uncomplicated ingredients of this raita belie the fabulous flavor of the mixture. It is particularly good as an accompaniment to a pulao or biriyani.

1 1/2 cups	plain yogurt	375 mL
2 cups	chopped tomatoes	500 mL
2	green onions, finely sliced with some green	2
1 tsp	minced green chilies, preferably serranos (optional)	5 mL
1/2 tsp	salt or to taste	2 mL
1/4 tsp	freshly ground black pepper or to taste	1 mL

1. Stir yogurt in a bowl until smooth and creamy. Stir in tomatoes, onions, chilies, if using, salt and pepper.
2. Cover and chill well before serving. (Can be refrigerated for up to 24 hours.)

Corn, Mango and Cucumber Raita

This is definitely one of my favorite summer raitas when green mangoes are plentiful. The tart mango is delicious with sweet summer corn, and the play of raisins and green chilies adds another level of taste. Crunchy peanuts complete the picture.

❋

1 cup	fresh or frozen corn kernels, thawed	250 mL
1 cup	diced peeled green (unripened) mango (1/4-inch/0.5 cm dice)	250 mL
1	cucumber, cut into 1/4-inch (0.5 cm) dice	1
1/4 cup	raisins	50 mL
3/4 cup	cilantro, chopped	175 mL
DRESSING		
2	cloves garlic	2
1	piece peeled gingerroot, 1 inch (2.5 cm)	1
1 to 2	green chilies, preferably serranos	1 to 2
1 1/2 cups	plain nonfat yogurt	375 mL
2 tsp	black salt (kala namak) or salt to taste	10 mL
1/2 tsp	granulated sugar	2 mL
1 tbsp	vegetable oil	15 mL
1 tsp	mustard seeds	5 mL
2 to 3	green chilies, preferably serranos, slivered	2 to 3
2 tsp	slivered peeled gingerroot	10 mL
1/3 cup	roasted peanuts, coarsely chopped	75 mL

1. In a large bowl, combine corn, mango, cucumber, raisins and cilantro.

2. *Dressing:* In a blender or food processor, purée garlic, ginger and whole chilies with 2 to 3 tbsp (25 to 45 mL) water to make a smooth paste. Stir into yogurt. Add salt and sugar. Pour dressing into vegetable and fruit mixture. Mix well. Cover and chill for up to 3 hours.

3. Just before serving, in a small saucepan, heat oil over high heat until very hot. Add mustard seeds and cover immediately. When popping stops within a few seconds, reduce heat to medium and add slivered chilies and ginger. Cook for 1 minute. Pour over raita. Stir in peanuts and serve.

Cabbage and Apple Raita

Serves 8 to 10

This versatile and substantial raita has accompanied many a company meal at my home. The texture and taste are unique yet go well with almost any food.

2 cups	plain yogurt	500 mL
3 tbsp	granulated sugar	45 mL
1 tsp	salt or to taste	5 mL
³⁄₄ tsp	freshly ground black pepper	4 mL
1 tbsp	freshly squeezed lemon juice	15 mL
2 cups	diced apples	500 mL
6 cups	very finely shredded cabbage	1.5 L
¹⁄₃ cup	roasted peanuts, chopped	75 mL
1 tbsp	vegetable oil	15 mL
1 ¹⁄₂ tsp	mustard seeds	7 mL

1. Stir yogurt in a bowl until smooth and creamy. Stir in sugar, salt and pepper. Cover and chill well before serving. (Can be refrigerated for up to 8 hours.)

2. In a separate bowl, toss together lemon juice and apples. Mix in cabbage. Cover and refrigerate until chilled or for up to 3 hours.

3. Just before serving, pour yogurt into cabbage mixture. Add peanuts and toss to mix well.

4. In a small saucepan, heat oil over high heat until almost smoking. Add mustard seeds and cover immediately. When seeds stop popping within a few seconds, pour over top of cabbage. Toss and serve immediately.

Palak Raita
Yogurt and Spinach with Five Seasonings

| | Serves 8 | |

Crushed mustard seeds are commonly used in water-based marinated vegetable pickles to add tang and color. Seldom have I seen them added uncooked to a dish as a seasoning. The unusual combination of uncooked spices, including asafetida, is what makes this raita outstanding. It is distinctive enough to stand on its own and makes a highly nutritious light lunch combined with one of the more substantial Indian breads, such as parathas.

✿

TIP
Crush mustard seeds in a spice grinder or with a mortar and pestle.

4 cups	plain yogurt	1 L
1 cup	well-drained chopped cooked spinach	250 mL
1 tsp	crushed mustard seeds (see Tip, left)	5 mL
½ tsp	cumin powder	2 mL
½ tsp	granulated sugar	2 mL
¼ tsp	asafetida (hing)	1 mL
¼ tsp	cayenne pepper	1 mL
¼ tsp	freshly ground black pepper	1 mL
¾ tsp	salt or to taste	4 mL

1. Stir yogurt in a bowl until smooth and creamy. Stir in spinach. Add mustard seeds, cumin, sugar, asafetida, cayenne pepper, black pepper and salt. Mix well.

2. Cover and chill well before serving. (Can be refrigerated for up to 3 days.)

Hari Chutney
Cilantro Mint Chutney

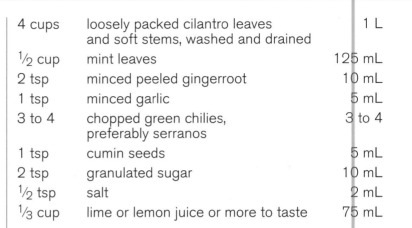

<table>
<tr><td>Makes 1 cup
(250 mL)</td></tr>
</table>

This chutney is a staple in most Indian homes. It is served as a dipping sauce with a multitude of Indian snacks and finger foods. It is also used as a sandwich spread.

❀

4 cups	loosely packed cilantro leaves and soft stems, washed and drained	1 L
1/2 cup	mint leaves	125 mL
2 tsp	minced peeled gingerroot	10 mL
1 tsp	minced garlic	5 mL
3 to 4	chopped green chilies, preferably serranos	3 to 4
1 tsp	cumin seeds	5 mL
2 tsp	granulated sugar	10 mL
1/2 tsp	salt	2 mL
1/3 cup	lime or lemon juice or more to taste	75 mL

1. In a blender, combine cilantro, mint, ginger, garlic, chilies, cumin seeds, sugar, salt and lime juice. Add 3 tbsp (45 mL) water and blend to a smooth paste, adding a little more water if necessary. Scrape sides of jar frequently to blend well. (Chutney can be stored in an airtight container in the refrigerator for up to 2 weeks or frozen for several months.)

Yogurt Mint Chutney

| Makes 1 cup |
| (250 mL) |

This rather runny chutney is always served as a dipping sauce with lamb kababs. It also makes a wonderful salad dressing.

❀

1 cup	plain yogurt, divided	250 mL
6 to 8	mint leaves	6 to 8
2 tbsp	cilantro	25 mL
1	green chili, preferably serrano	1
1/4 tsp	salt or to taste	1 mL

1. In a blender, combine 1/4 cup (50 mL) of the yogurt, mint, cilantro, chili and salt. Blend into a smooth paste. Transfer to a bowl. Stir into remaining yogurt.
2. Cover and chill before serving. (Chutney can be stored in an airtight container in the refrigerator for up to 1 week. Do not freeze.)

Date and Peanut Chutney

This wonderful sweet chutney is great to include on a condiment tray. As well, with the addition of one or two different seasonings, it can be transformed into an unusual barbecue or basting sauce. I have added a healthy dose of Asian sambal. The result is dynamite!

※

TIP

Jaggery is unrefined cane sugar and tastes like molasses. Substitute ½ cup (125 mL) molasses if unable to obtain jaggery.

½ cup	raw peanuts, skinless	125 mL
16 to 20	cloves garlic	16 to 20
1	piece peeled gingerroot (2 inches/5 cm), chopped	1
1½ tbsp	cayenne pepper	22 mL
8 oz	chopped dates	250 g
2 cups	cider vinegar, divided	500 mL
½ cup	jaggery (gur), cut into pieces (see Tip, left)	125 mL
½ tsp	salt or to taste	2 mL
2 to 3 tbsp	Asian sambal or to taste	25 to 45 mL

1. In a blender, grind peanuts until powdery. Add garlic, ginger, cayenne pepper and dates. Purée with ¾ cup (175 mL) of the vinegar to make a smooth paste.

2. Transfer paste to a saucepan. Add jaggery, salt and remaining vinegar. Mix well. Cook over medium heat, stirring, until mixture bubbles and thickens, 12 to 15 minutes.

3. Let cool to room temperature. Add sambal to taste. (Chutney can be stored in an airtight container in the refrigerator for up to 2 weeks. Do not freeze.)

Tamarind Chutney

*This sweet-sour chutney
is more like a sauce,
and there are many
regional variations.
The base is tamarind,
a very sour pod 3 to
4 inches (7.5 to 10 cm)
long. The tamarind tree
grows in many parts
of India and also in
Mexico. For this sauce,
use the compressed
slab-like tamarind
available in Asian
stores, not the "instant"
kind. The fresh pods
available in grocery
stores are not suitable
for this recipe.*

❊

TIP

To make tamarind water:
Cut 1-inch (2.5 cm)
strip from tamarind
slab, about 2 oz (60 g).
Break into smaller pieces
and soak in 1¼ cups
(300 mL) hot water for
30 minutes. Soften
between fingers to make
a pulp. Strain through
large-holed strainer into
bowl, pushing with
back of spoon to
extract as much pulp
as possible. Discard rest.

1 cup	tamarind water (see Tip, left)	250 mL
¾ cup	chopped dates or	175 mL
	½ cup (125 mL) jaggery (gur)	
1 tsp	cayenne pepper	5 mL
½ tsp	cumin powder	2 mL
½ tsp	salt or to taste	2 mL

1. In a saucepan over medium heat, combine tamarind water and dates. Bring to a boil. Reduce heat to medium-low and cook until mixture begins to thicken, 5 to 8 minutes. After mixture has thickened, mash with a spoon.

2. Add cayenne pepper, cumin, salt and ¾ cup (175 mL) water. Simmer for 5 minutes to allow flavors to blend.

3. Press through large-holed strainer to make a thick, smooth sauce-like chutney. Let cool to room temperature and serve as a dipping sauce with appetizers. (Chutney can be stored in an airtight container in the refrigerator for several months. Do not freeze.)

Hot Pineapple Chutney

Makes 2 cups (500 mL)		

A tasty accompaniment to a lightly seasoned meal, this chutney can also be served with finger foods. I particularly like it with pork.

3 cups	diced pineapple, preferably sweet variety called Gold (1/2-inch/1 cm dice)	750 mL
2 tsp	salt	10 mL
2 1/2 tbsp	cayenne pepper	32 mL
1 tsp	turmeric	5 mL
1/2 tsp	ground fenugreek seeds (methi) or more to taste	2 mL
1/4 tsp	asafetida (hing) or more to taste	1 mL
1/3 cup	vegetable oil	75 mL
1 tsp	mustard seeds	5 mL

1. In a bowl, combine pineapple and salt. Set aside.

2. In another bowl, combine cayenne pepper, turmeric, fenugreek and asafetida.

3. In a medium saucepan, heat oil over high heat until a couple of mustard seeds thrown in start to sputter. Add remaining mustard seeds and cover immediately. Uncover in a few seconds when seeds stop popping. Reduce heat to medium. Add spice mix. Stir-fry for 10 seconds. Add pineapple. Cook, maintaining a gentle boil the entire time, stirring frequently, until mixture is thick, about 10 minutes.

4. Cover and serve at room temperature or chill before serving. (Chutney can be stored in an airtight container in the refrigerator for up to 2 weeks. Do not freeze.)

Sweet Mango Chutney

This quintessential mango chutney is synonymous with Indian food.

TIP

This chutney is usually made once a year at the beginning of the mango season, when the best unripe mangoes are available. It is made in large quantities and stored at room temperature to last until the next season. It will keep for years, even though it darkens with age.

2 lbs	green (unripened) mangoes	1 kg
3 tbsp	salt	45 mL
1¾ cups	granulated sugar	425 mL
1	large head garlic, cloves peeled and lightly smashed	1
1 tbsp	cayenne pepper	15 mL
1 tsp	ginger powder	5 mL
1 tsp	nigella seeds (kalaunji)	5 mL
1 tsp	cumin seeds	5 mL
½ tsp	black peppercorns	2 mL
½ cup	cider vinegar, divided	125 mL

1. Peel mangoes. Holding each vertically with stem end up, slice down both sides with a very sharp knife, as close to the seed as possible. Lay each side on a board, flat side down, and cut into 4 long pieces. Cut the fleshy portion along both sides of the pit and discard pit.

2. Place mango slices in a glass or non-reactive dish. Sprinkle with salt and rub in well with fingers to coat pieces. Cover and set in the sun for 3 to 4 hours. Drain mangoes and set aside.

3. In a saucepan over low heat, dissolve sugar in ½ cup (125 mL) water. Add mangoes, garlic, cayenne pepper, ginger, nigella and cumin seeds and peppercorns. Increase heat to medium-low and cook, stirring occasionally until mixture thickens, 15 to 20 minutes. Do not mash mango slices.

4. Add ¼ cup (50 mL) of the vinegar and stir gently. When absorbed, stir in remaining vinegar. Cook for 2 minutes longer or until absorbed.

5. Let cool to room temperature and store in a bottle.

Sweets and Beverages

THROUGHOUT MY YEARS of teaching, I have frequently heard the comment that Indian sweets are too sweet. Conversely, Indians seem to find Western desserts too sweet and rich. My view is that it is a different kind of sweetness, and over a period of time and with frequent exposure, the palate gets more attuned to, and therefore more accepting of, the difference. Also, it is a fact that Indian desserts contain unusual ingredients, not the familiar eggs, butter, flour, sugar, chocolate and cream. The results are obviously very different in appearance, texture and taste, and not always acceptable to all.

I have picked the tried-and-true favorites. Most are simple everyday desserts that are perfect endings for an Indian meal. The selection also demonstrates the diversity of ingredients — grains, yogurt, milk, nuts and vegetables.

Indian drinks, too, are unusual. Lassi, the cooling yogurt drink, is my favorite. I had never encountered mango lassi until we moved to the United States, but now it is by far the most popular of the lassi drinks. Nimbu pani, or lemonade, used to be served to visitors and guests who dropped in for a visit, until sodas came crashing into our culture. Now nimbu pani is considered old-fashioned.

But chai (tea) reigns supreme. Indians are passionate about their cup of chai, plain or masala (spiced), but until recently, always hot. Iced tea has just arrived in India, and is already the drink most popular with young people.

❋ ❋ ❋

Kheer

North Indian Rice Pudding

Serves 6 to 8		

A traditional North Indian favorite, this dessert depends on the slow reduction of milk, a very important technique in the making of milk desserts. The milk flavor is intensified as natural sugars are concentrated, and takes on a complexity that is unique.

❊

TIPS

Pudding can be made up to 2 days ahead and refrigerated.

◆

Silver varak is a very thin film of sterling silver. It is edible and is used to garnish special sweets and rice dishes. It is readily available in cake decorating supply stores.

◆

Recipe can be halved. It will take less time to thicken, about 1 hour.

8 cups	whole milk	2 L
8	green cardamom pods, slightly crushed	8
2 tbsp	long-grain rice	25 mL
4 to 5 tbsp	granulated sugar	60 to 75 mL
3 tbsp	chopped unsalted pistachios, divided	45 mL
1 to 2	sheets edible silver leaf (varak) (see Tips, left) (optional)	1 to 2

1. In a large heavy-bottomed saucepan over medium to medium–high heat, combine milk, cardamom and rice. (Do not use a nonstick pan.) Bring to a boil. Reduce heat immediately to maintain a gentle boil. This is critical. Every 5 to 6 minutes, a layer of cream and froth will form on top. Gently stir this in and mix well. Periodically scrape bottom of pan to make sure milk is not scorching.

2. Reduce by half. This will take $1\frac{1}{2}$ to 2 hours, stirring every 5 to 6 minutes. (Watch more closely as the mixture reduces. You don't want it to burn.) Remove from heat. Remove cardamom pods, if desired.

3. Stir in sugar to taste and 2 tbsp (25 mL) of the pistachios. Mix well. Let cool.

4. Mix again and pour into serving bowl. Let cool to room temperature. Pudding will be the texture of pancake batter at this point and will thicken to the consistency of chocolate sauce when chilled.

5. Garnish with silver leaf sheets, if using, by carefully inverting tissue-backed sheets over surface of pudding. Do not handle sheets directly with your fingers as they are fragile. Sprinkle with remaining nuts.

6. Cover bowl with plastic wrap and chill well before serving.

Date and Nut Pinwheels

*These pinwheels are
wonderful served with
tea or coffee or, if
you prefer, as dessert
with a dollop of
whipped cream.*

2 cups	packed chopped dates	500 mL
½ cup	finely chopped raw cashews	125 mL
1 cup	sweetened flaked or shredded coconut, divided	250 mL

1. Wrap dates in plastic wrap and place on a cutting board. Mash with a rolling pin or a wooden mallet or pulse in a food processor until they form a paste and hold together.

2. Place another large piece of plastic wrap, about 16 inches (40 cm) long, on table with the short end facing you. Spoon dates lengthwise down middle in a line about 10 inches (25 cm) long. Cover with second piece of plastic wrap. Flatten with hand into as even a rectangle as possible. With rolling pin, roll into even rectangle about 13 by 8 inches (32 by 20 cm), lifting wrap and flipping over occasionally to eliminate wrinkles.

3. Turn so long end faces you. Remove upper plastic wrap. Sprinkle date surface evenly with cashews, leaving a ¼-inch (0.5 cm) border on far long edge. Top with ½ cup (125 mL) of the coconut. Starting at edge closest to you, with the help of plastic wrap carefully form into a roll, peeling off plastic wrap as you roll and pressing to compact. Pinch edge to seal.

4. On another piece of plastic wrap, sprinkle remaining coconut. Carefully transfer roll onto coconut and roll to cover dates completely. Roll up tightly in plastic wrap, twisting ends to enclose. Refrigerate for at least 3 hours or for up to 2 days.

5. With a sharp knife, cut into approximately ½-inch (1 cm) thick slices. (Cut straight down. Do not use sawing motion.)

Byculla Bread and Butter Pudding

This dessert comes from the Anglo-Indian community of Mumbai and it is named for the area Byculla, where many of them lived. It is by far one of the best bread and butter puddings I have ever eaten.

TIP

Rose essence is not to be confused with rose water. It is rose extract, but known as "essence." It has an indefinite shelf life and is available in Indian markets.

◆ *Preheat oven to 400°F (200°C)*
◆ *8-inch (2 L) square baking dish, generously greased with butter*

¾ cup	granulated sugar	175 mL
4 cups	whole milk	1 L
4	extra-large eggs	4
2 tbsp	granulated sugar	25 mL
½ tsp	vanilla	2 mL
¼ tsp	rose essence (see Tip, left)	1 mL
1½ tsp	freshly grated nutmeg	7 mL
½ tsp	cardamom powder	2 mL
¼ cup	butter, softened	50 mL
8	slices firm white bread, crusts trimmed	8
¼ cup	good-quality orange marmalade	50 mL
4 tbsp	sliced almonds, divided	60 mL
2 tbsp	raisins	25 mL

1. Dust prepared dish with ¾ cup (175 mL) sugar to coat all sides. Shake out any excess sugar and discard. Set aside.

2. In a heavy saucepan, bring milk to a boil over medium heat. (Do not use a nonstick pan.) Reduce heat to maintain a gentle boil, stirring frequently to mix cream and froth as it rises back into the milk. Try to keep side of pan as clean as possible. Reduce to 2 to 2¼ cups (500 to 550 mL). This will take about 30 minutes. Let cool slightly.

3. Beat eggs, adding 2 tbsp (25 mL) sugar in 3 to 4 batches, until light and foamy. Gradually pour warm milk into eggs, stirring to mix. Stir in vanilla, rose essence, nutmeg and cardamom.

4. Butter one side of each bread slice. Spread 4 buttered slices with marmalade. Place in prepared baking dish, marmalade side up, overlapping as necessary. Sprinkle with 2 tbsp (25 mL) of the almonds and raisins. Cover with remaining 4 bread slices, buttered side down. Pour egg mixture on top. Gently press down with spatula, making sure top of bread is covered. Garnish with remaining almonds.

5. Bake in preheated oven for 10 minutes. Reduce heat to 350°F (180°C) and bake for 15 to 20 minutes longer or until toothpick inserted in center comes out clean. If necessary, brown under broiler for a few minutes until top is golden and crisp. Serve warm, at room temperature or chilled.

Almond Halwa

Makes 20 pieces

Nutmeg adds an interesting twist to this simple dessert, which is often served as part of an assortment of Indian finger sweets, with tea and coffee. This fudge-like sweet is not the same as the halva made with sesame seeds and honey that is available in Jewish and Middle Eastern delis.

TIP

Work quickly once mixture is transferred to pan as it sets quickly and almonds will fall off if too cool.

◆ *8-inch (2 L) square cake pan, greased*

6 tbsp	butter	90 mL
½ cup	fine semolina (sooji)	125 mL
1 cup plus 2 tbsp	ground almonds	250 mL plus 25 mL
½ cup	granulated sugar	125 mL
1 ¼ tsp	freshly ground nutmeg	6 mL
1 ⅓ cups	whole or 2% milk	325 mL
2 tbsp	sliced almonds	25 mL

1. In a heavy saucepan or wok, melt butter over medium heat. Stir in semolina and cook, stirring, until golden, 3 to 4 minutes.

2. Add ground almonds, sugar and nutmeg. Mix well. Add milk, about ¼ cup (50 mL) at a time, and stir to incorporate. Mixture will thicken and pull away from side of saucepan.

3. Remove from heat and quickly spread evenly in prepared pan. Press sliced almonds into top of halwa and let cool. Cut into diamonds or squares. Refrigerate for at least 1 hour before removing from pan. (Can be refrigerated in an airtight container for up to 3 days.)

Orange Saffron Pudding

I call this dish "breakfast for dinner," and it always evokes gasps. The plainest of breakfast ingredients are transformed into an amazingly soul-satisfying and healthy dessert in minutes.

TIPS

The dessert looks elegant and impressive if set in a glass bowl. Make up to 24 hours ahead and keep covered in the refrigerator.

Although most of my recipes use whole or 2% milk, in this recipe you can use skim, if you prefer.

You can use whatever variety of cream of wheat cereal you prefer, including instant. There is so much milk used here in proportion to the cream of wheat that it won't turn into a gooey mess.

2 cups	milk, divided (see Tips, left)	500 mL
1/2 tsp	saffron threads	2 mL
1 tbsp	butter	15 mL
1 tbsp	slivered almonds	15 mL
1 tbsp	raisins	15 mL
1/3 cup	cream of wheat cereal (see Tips, left)	75 mL
1/4 tsp	crushed cardamom seeds	1 mL
1 tsp	grated orange rind	5 mL
3/4 cup	granulated sugar	175 mL
1/2 cup	freshly squeezed orange juice	125 mL
1	can (10 oz/284 mL) mandarin orange slices, drained	1

1. In a microwave-safe bowl, microwave 1/4 cup (50 mL) of the milk on High until very hot. Add saffron. Set aside for 15 minutes.

2. Melt butter in a large wok or nonstick saucepan over medium heat. Stir-fry almonds and raisins for 1 minute. Add cream of wheat. Stir-fry until golden, about 2 minutes.

3. Remove from heat. Add remaining milk, saffron milk, cardamom and orange rind, whisking well to make sure there are no lumps. Return to medium heat. Cook, stirring continuously, until thickened like pancake batter, 6 to 8 minutes.

4. Add sugar and orange juice. Mixture will loosen and curdle slightly but will become smooth again as it cooks. Continue to stir and simmer until mixture thickens again, 6 to 8 minutes. Pour into a heatproof serving dish and let set as it cools.

5. Chill well, about 30 minutes. Decorate with mandarin slices.

Heavenly Saffron Yogurt Cheese

Serves 8		

The signature sweet of Gujerat, this dish is stunning in its simplicity. The slight tanginess of the yogurt combined with the sugar and saffron results in a heavenly taste and creamy texture, but it is relatively fat-free. It is often served with puris, light puffy fried bread, but it also makes a wonderful accompaniment to fresh fruit as a substitute for whipped cream.

TIP

This dish can be made ahead up to Step 3, then covered and refrigerated for up to 2 days. Garnish with nuts just before serving.

8 cups	plain nonfat yogurt, divided	2 L
¾ tsp	saffron threads	4 mL
2 tbsp	hot milk	25 mL
2 cups	granulated sugar	500 mL
¼ cup	chopped raw pistachios	50 mL

1. Divide yogurt into 2 equal portions. Place each portion in a double layer of cheesecloth and tie tightly. Place in a colander set over a bowl, making sure that the cheesecloth does not soak in the liquid. Refrigerate for 5 to 6 hours or overnight until liquid has drained from yogurt.

2. Soak saffron in hot milk for 15 minutes.

3. Transfer drained yogurt to a large bowl and gradually beat in sugar with a wooden spoon or spatula until smooth and lump-free. Do not put in blender. Add saffron milk and mix well.

4. Spoon into individual dishes. Sprinkle with nuts and chill for several hours before serving.

Gajar ka Halwa
Caramelized Carrot Pudding

Serves 8		

This is a favorite in north India and is particularly good when made with the sweet pink winter carrots grown in that area. The flavor is more delicate than other carrots, and they are juicier. I have never come across this variety in North America.

❋

TIP

This dish freezes well for several months. Thaw and warm in a 200°F (100°C) oven. Sprinkle with additional almonds and top with edible silver, if using.

1 ½ lbs	carrots, grated (5 or 6)	750 g
4 cups	whole milk	1 L
1 ¼ cups	granulated sugar (approx.)	300 mL
¼ cup	vegetable oil or unsalted butter	50 mL
¼ cup	raisins	50 mL
8 to 10	cardamom pods	8 to 10
	Blanched whole almonds	
	Edible silver leaf (varak) (see Tips, page 172) (optional)	

1. In a large heavy-bottomed saucepan over medium heat, combine carrots and milk. Cook, stirring frequently, until milk is completely absorbed and mixture begins to solidify, about 1 hour.

2. Stir in 1 cup (250 mL) of the sugar, oil and raisins. When sugar dissolves, check sweetness. Add remaining sugar if needed. Cook, stirring constantly, until mixture begins to leave side of pan, 15 to 20 minutes.

3. Remove seeds from cardamom pods, discarding pods. Pound seeds and stir into pudding. Serve warm or at room temperature. Before serving, garnish with blanched almonds and top with edible silver leaf, if using (see North Indian Rice Pudding, page 172, for directions on using).

SWEETS AND BEVERAGES **179**

Shahi Tukre
Royal Bread Pudding

<table>
<tr><td colspan="3">◆ 8-cup (2 L) baking dish, sprayed with vegetable spray</td></tr>
<tr><td>2 cups</td><td>light (5%) cream, divided</td><td>500 mL</td></tr>
<tr><td>½ tsp</td><td>saffron threads</td><td>2 mL</td></tr>
<tr><td>¾ cup</td><td>granulated sugar</td><td>175 mL</td></tr>
<tr><td></td><td>Vegetable oil</td><td></td></tr>
<tr><td>1</td><td>loaf French bread,
preferably the softer variety</td><td>1</td></tr>
<tr><td>2 cups</td><td>whole or 2% milk (approx.)</td><td>500 mL</td></tr>
<tr><td>2 tbsp</td><td>granulated sugar</td><td>25 mL</td></tr>
<tr><td>½ tsp</td><td>crushed cardamom seeds or powder</td><td>2 mL</td></tr>
<tr><td>2 tbsp</td><td>sliced almonds, toasted</td><td>25 mL</td></tr>
</table>

Serves 6 to 8

A classic among Moghul desserts, this elegant bread pudding is a favorite at Muslim weddings and celebrations.

❋

1. In a microwave-safe bowl, heat ¼ cup (50 mL) of the cream on High until very hot. Drop saffron into cream and set aside for 15 minutes.

2. In a saucepan over low heat, combine ¾ cup (175 mL) sugar and 1½ cups (375 mL) water. Stir until sugar is dissolved. Keep warm.

3. Pour enough oil into a skillet to come ½ inch (1 cm) up the side. Heat over medium heat.

4. Cut bread into 1-inch (2.5 cm) thick slices. In batches, dip each slice quickly into milk and carefully place in hot oil. Fry both sides until golden brown, 2 to 3 minutes. Do not crowd skillet.

5. With a slotted spoon, carefully remove each slice from skillet and dip quickly into sugar syrup. Arrange in layer in prepared dish. Repeat with remaining bread slices, layering as necessary.

6. Meanwhile, in another saucepan over medium-low heat, reduce remaining cream by about one-third, 10 to 12 minutes. Stir in 2 tbsp (25 mL) sugar, reserved saffron with cream, and cardamom. Stir and pour over bread.

7. Garnish with almonds. Cover and refrigerate for several hours before serving or for up to 24 hours.

Mango Kulfi

*Mango is the national
fruit of India, and there
are more than 200
varieties grown in the
country. Every Indian
attests to a regional
variety being the best.
For kulfi, however,
canned mango purée is
the best. All brands are
made from the variety
known as Alphonso
(named after the
Portuguese ruler), and
it is indisputably the
king of mangoes.*

TIP

Kulfi moulds are
individual aluminum
cone-shaped containers
with a screw-on cover.
Kulfi can also be set
in 3 empty 14-oz
(398 mL) cans. Dip can
momentarily into warm
water and run knife
around inside of can to
loosen. Slide out kulfi
into a dish and slice
$\frac{1}{2}$ inch (1 cm) thick.
Serve garnished with
pistachios. Plastic
Popsicle moulds are
also suitable (without
inserting the stick).

◆ *Kulfi moulds (see Tip, left)*

4 cups	whole milk	1 L
1	can (14 oz/398 mL) sweetened condensed milk or 1¾ cups (425 mL)	1
½ tsp	cardamom seeds, powdered	2 mL
2 cups	canned Indian mango purée	500 mL
3 tbsp	unsalted pistachios, skinned and chopped	45 mL
	Fresh mango slices (optional)	

1. In a large saucepan over medium heat, combine milk and condensed milk. (Do not use a nonstick pan.) Bring to a boil, stirring well to combine. Add cardamom powder. Cook, stirring frequently to prevent scorching, until mixture is reduced by about one-third, 25 to 30 minutes. Stir in mango purée.

2. Pour into a shallow container and freeze until just set. Beat with a fork or immersion blender to break up ice crystals. Repeat procedure once more.

3. Pack mixture into kulfi moulds or any suitable moulds and freeze.

4. Run knife around inside of mould. Dip mould momentarily in warm water and slip kulfi into an individual serving dish. Garnish with a few pistachios. Serve with diced fresh mangoes when in season.

Lassi

Savory Yogurt Cooler

Serves 4

Lassi is the summer drink in India, either sweet or savory. My personal favorite is definitely the savory version, cool and refreshing, with the aroma of fresh ground cumin.

1 tsp	cumin seeds	5 mL
2 cups	plain yogurt	500 mL
¾ tsp	salt or to taste	4 mL
½ tsp	freshly ground black pepper or to taste	2 mL

1. Toast cumin seeds in a small skillet over medium heat until seeds turn a shade darker and aromatic, about 3 minutes. Let cool and grind with mortar and pestle or in spice grinder until powdery. Set aside.

2. In a blender, combine yogurt, 2 cups (500 mL) cold water and 1 to 2 cups (250 to 500 mL) ice cubes. Add salt, pepper and half the cumin powder and blend until smooth.

3. Pour into 4 tall glasses to serve. Sprinkle with remaining cumin to garnish.

Sweet Lassi

Sweet Yogurt Cooler

Serves 4

2 cups	plain yogurt	500 mL
2 to 3 tbsp	sugar or to taste	25 to 45 mL
Pinch	salt	Pinch

1. In a blender, combine yogurt, sugar, salt, 2 cups (500 mL) cold water and 1 to 2 cups (250 to 500 mL) ice cubes. Blend until smooth.

2. Pour into 4 tall glasses to serve.

Mango Lassi

Serves 4

I had never had mango lassi until I came to the United States, but it is a favorite in restaurants now. I prefer to use canned Indian mango purée as mangoes are seasonal and only the sweetest fiber-free ones should be used.

❋

1 1/2 cups	plain yogurt	375 mL
1 1/2 cups	canned Indian mango purée or to taste	375 mL
1/2 cup	whole or 2% milk	125 mL

1. In a blender, combine yogurt, mango purée, milk and 1 to 2 cups (250 to 500 mL) ice cubes and blend until smooth.
2. Pour into 4 tall glasses to serve.

Masala Chai
Spiced Tea

This is my favorite recipe for masala chai (spiced tea), an ancient Indian tradition. Many variations abound, but basically it is made with black tea leaves and aromatic spices and herbs and is astonishingly soul-satisfying. It is also healing and soothing, depending on the spices used. The addition of ginger is particularly good for a cold or queasy stomach.

❋

TIP

If making 4 cups (1 L) or more at a time, reduce tea to ¾ tsp (4 mL) per cup.

½ cup	milk (any type)	125 mL
2	whole cloves	2
1	green cardamom pod, one side peeled open	1
1	thin slice peeled gingerroot, about ½ inch (1 cm) round	1
4 to 5	pieces (2 inches/5 cm) lemongrass (optional)	4 to 5
2 tsp	Indian black tea leaves	10 mL
2 tsp	granulated sugar or to taste	10 mL

1. In a saucepan over medium-high heat, combine 1½ cups (375 mL) water, milk, cloves, cardamom, ginger and lemongrass, if using. Bring to a boil.

2. Add tea and sugar. Reduce heat to medium and simmer for 2 minutes. Remove from heat, cover and let tea steep for 3 to 4 minutes longer. (If using an electric stove, turn off heat, cover and leave on burner.) Strain into warmed teapot or into cups.

National Library of Canada Cataloguing in Publication

Vaswani, Suneeta
    Easy Indian cooking / Suneeta Vaswani.

ISBN 0-7788-0088-1

1. Cookery, Indian. I. Title.

TX724.5.I4V38 2004   641.5954   C2003-906490-5

Mail Order Sources

Patel Bros.
5815 Hillcroft
Houston, TX 77036
713-784-8332

There are many stores throughout the United States with this name, but they are all independently owned. This one has been in business for more than 20 years and is the primary mail order source for Indians in the south and southeast United States.

Kalustyan's
123 Lexington Avenue
New York, NY 10016
800-352-3451
www.kalustyans.com

A famous New York source that has been handling international foods for half a century or longer.

Penzey's Spices
Multiple locations
414-679-7207 or 800-741-7787
www.penzeys.com

Premier family-owned and operated spice company with an outstanding mail order business and retail stores in 10 states. The quarterly catalogs, packed with detailed information and recipes, are worth saving.

Website Shopping

Indian Foods Co.
www.Indianfoodsco.com

One-stop shopping for everything from chutneys to herbs and spices to cookbooks.

Get Spice
The online spice shop
www.getspice.com

Very easy-to-use website. Spices listed with color photos. Teas, kitchen equipment and cookbooks also available.

Ethnic Grocers
www.ethnicgrocer.com

Herbs and spices, oils, sauces, teas and much more available here. Free catalog available upon request.

Index